Tutoring and Mentoring

*Starting a Peer Helping Program
in Your Elementary School*

Nancy Keim
with
Cindy Tolliver

Resource Publications, Inc.

To Connie Besancon

Editorial director: Kenneth Guentert
Managing editor: Elizabeth J. Asborno
Illustrator: Diane Guelzow
Cover design and production: Huey Lee
Cover photographs: Nancy Keim

Reprint Department
Resource Publications, Inc.
160 East Virginia Street #290
San Jose, CA 95112-5876

Library of Congress Cataloging in Publication Data
Keim, Nancy, 1950-
    Tutoring and mentoring : starting a peer-helping program in your
    elementary school / Nancy Keim with Cindy Tolliver.
        p.   cm.
    Includes bibliographical references.
    ISBN 0-89390-259-4 : $14.95
    1. Peer-group tutoring of students—United States.   2. Mentors in
    education—United States.   3. Education, Elementary—United
    States.   I. Tolliver, Cindy, 1951-   . II. Title.
    LB1031.5.K45   1993
    372.14—dc20   93-8

97 96 95 94 93 | 5 4 3 2 1

The IALAC activity found in Form B-4 in Appendix B is adapted from
Sidney Simon, *I Am Lovable and Capable: A Modern Allegory on the
Classical Put-Down,* ©1991 Values Press, Hadley, Massachussetts.

The statistical data found in Chapter 3, "A Peer Helping Success
Story," and the Evaluations (Forms C-1 through C-3) in Appendix C
are adapted from Mary Fox, "Evaluation of The Westwood
Elementary Peer Helper Program," Master's thesis, San Diego State
University, 1992.

"Do's and Don'ts for Peer Helpers" and "Peer Helper's Code of
Ethics" (Forms B-8 and B-9 in Appendix B) are adapted from *Ethics
and Standards for Peer Counseling Professionals and Peer Counselors,* ©
1990 California Peer Counseling Association.

Contents

Part Four: Managing a Successful Program

Part Five: Troubleshooting

Appendix A: Forms for Planning and Initiating Your Peer Helping Program

Appendix B: Forms for Training Peer Helpers

Appendix C: Forms for Evaluating Your Program

Acknowledgments

Many people have assisted me in my efforts. I particularly want to thank Cathy Moran of Poway High School, whose commitment to the peer helping process inspired me and whose guidance in the early development of the Peer Helping program at Westwood Elementary, San Diego, California, was invaluable. Thanks to my family and friends, who encouraged me to challenge myself. Thanks also to Sam Blank for his guidance and to the staff and parents at Westwood for their openness and support of the program.

A special thanks to Karen Garappolo for her artistic contributions.

Finally, I want to express my appreciation to all the peer helpers whose hard work and dedication has helped hundreds of younger children and whose success made this book possible.

Preface

The concept of peers helping peers has been in the educational spotlight in recent years. More and more schools across the nation have tested programs utilizing older children to teach specific subjects and/or social skills to younger schoolmates. Well-run cross-age helping programs—variously called "peer helping," "peer mentoring," "peer counseling," "peer tutoring," etc.—have proven to be tremendously popular. They provide a way for the growing number of students who need one-on-one help to get the extra attention they need, in spite of overcrowded classrooms and overworked teachers.

Children helping children may not seem like anything new. After all, the method has been used in one-room schools, in large families and in regular classrooms on an informal basis for years. What is new and exciting, however, is the training that the older children, or the peer helpers, receive, allowing them to more effectively and consistently help their younger peers. In addition to valuable training in interpersonal skills, the formalized structure of this program supports and recognizes helpers for their valuable contribution.

This book is intended for anyone—teacher, counselor, administrator, parent or community volunteer, or community social worker—interested in organizing and implementing a peer helping program in an elementary school. It focuses on two complementary types of peer helping: tutoring and mentoring. It is based on my personal experience in designing and implementing such a program at Westwood Elementary School in San Diego, California.

The book has three broad purposes:

1. To provide a step-by-step procedure for customizing my model for a peer helping program to fit your school's needs.

2. To provide procedures for implementing your proposed program.

3. To help you manage the program successfully once it is up and running.

Using the Model in this Book

This book was designed to be a complete guide for making your school's peer helping program successful. I recommend that you first read it in its entirety to get a general picture of what's involved; then go back and work through the process piece by piece. As you read, you may want to use the wide right margin to jot down notes and ideas. Bear in mind that reading about this complex process is a little like reading a detailed narrative of how to make a peanut-butter-and-jelly sandwich—it sounds much more complicated than it really is. Once you start actually doing it, the pieces seem to fall into place.

The diagram on the next page shows an overview of the process. The book's overall organization is based upon the flow of this process.

Part One, "Introduction to Peer Helping," defines peer helping and peer helpers. It outlines the benefits of peer helping, then relates the success of the model program at Westwood Elementary.

Part Two, "Planning," describes the steps you need to go through before starting your program. It includes information on how to assess the needs of your school; it presents a checklist of decisions you need to make to design a proposal based on those needs; and it suggests how to gain administrative and staff support for your proposal.

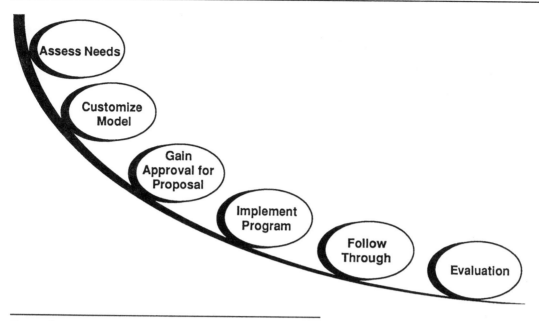

Organizational Process for Peer Helping Program

Part Three, "Customizing the Model," is the longest section. It presents a basic model of a peer helping program and describes options for various elements including scheduling, selection of peer helpers, training, staff responsibilities, and the matching up of helpers with helpees. From this information you will be able to pick and choose what will work best in your school.

Part Four, "Managing a Successful Peer Helping Program," details how to manage your program including communications between entities in the program, scheduling problems, personnel needs, evaluations, the development of new peer helping projects, and budget considerations.

Part Five, "Troubleshooting," discusses potential pitfalls and how to avoid them.

The appendices provide useful information and documents you will use along the way. For your convenience, these materials are marked with the "PEERS" symbol to the right, which means they are permissible to photocopy. As the acrostic illustrates, "PEERS" is an acronym for "Positive, Energetic, Enthusiastic, Responsible Students."

The Resources section provides you with a list of recommended books on related topics and the addresses of companies where you can obtain tutoring and mentoring materials for your program.

PEERS

P – Positive
E – Energetic
E – Enthusiastic
R – Responsible
S – Students

Additionally, I am available to help you start your peer helping program. To contact me about scheduling a presentation or workshop in your school or district, write to the address below. Your inquiry will be forwarded to me, and I will contact you (include your phone number in your letter).

Nancy Keim
Resource Publications, Inc.
160 E. Virginia Street #290-AWR
San Jose, CA 95112-5876

Part One

Introduction to Peer Helping

*I get by with a little
help from my friends.*
—The Beatles

1. What Is Peer Helping?

Peer helping is a formal process in which caring older students help younger students by tutoring them in specific subjects, by role-modeling good social skills, or by just being a special friend. An older student who has received training in helping peers is called a **peer helper**; the younger student receiving help is called the **helpee**. These two students meet once or twice a week. The peer helpers themselves meet with each other regularly to discuss successes and/or problems they have with their helpees.

Two Types of Peer Helpers: Tutors and Mentors

This book's model covers two types of peer helpers: peer tutors and peer mentors. The two complement each other in forming a complete school helping program.

- A **peer tutor** assists younger students with areas in the school curriculum including reading, spelling, writing, mathematics, penmanship, ESL, science, and computers. Tutoring usually takes place in a classroom.

- A **peer mentor** assists others in developing good social skills by serving as a positive role-model. Peer mentors also work on issues such as learning to be part of a group, playing fairly, showing respect, and resolving conflicts. Mentoring usually takes place on the playground, often in an area where children come together to engage in various games under the peer mentor's guidance.

A peer helper may want to be both a tutor and a mentor. Or he or she may be a tutor one semester and a mentor the next. Often, the choice to be a tutor or mentor is determined by the needs of the younger students in a particular school. Therefore, it is important that all peer helpers receive training in both tutoring and mentoring.

All peer helpers work with the **peer helper advisor** and the **receiving teachers** (the helpees' teachers), both of whom assess needs and check progress. **Sending teachers** (the helpers' teachers) support the program by allowing their students to leave class early, if necessary, to provide tutoring or mentoring. See chapters 19 and 20 for more about the sending and receiving teachers' responsibilities.

2. Why Peer Helping Works

Peer helpers have a unique teaching tool: Because they are close to the age of the helpees, they can talk their language. Thus they have more credibility as an ally in learning than does an adult authority figure who seems to be miles away in attitudes and years. The more relaxed atmosphere between peers results in a helpee who is less anxious and more open to new ideas; in other words, he or she is more "teachable."

Benefits of Peer Helping

Peer helping meets the needs of all concerned: helpees, helpers, and teachers. The benefits to the helpees are clear. First of all, they receive much-needed individualized help with schoolwork, and they have fun as they learn. Slower learners are encouraged, gifted ones are challenged, and that often overlooked group in the middle are paid the attention they richly deserve. Another positive experience for helpees is that they feel liked and accepted by an older schoolmate, which enhances their self-confidence. A self-confident student performs better in school and is less "at risk" of dropping out later. Younger children also benefit by working with positive role-models who can show them the ropes and the way to make it in a competitive grade-school world. A positive role-model at an early age, as seen in the Big Brother and Big Sister programs, can make a significant difference in a youngster's life. Finally, children of all ages need all the friends they can get.

Benefits to the peer helpers are an interesting and unexpected bonus. First of all, as helpers teach helpees, their own grasp of a subject improves as they bone up on fractions and phonetics. Older children who themselves have learning difficulties gain confidence in their own abilities; they will feel like experts to a child three years younger. Older children benefit by feeling useful, influential and appreciated. They want and need to make an important contribution. Being peer helpers is a way to experience themselves as people who have something valuable to give. Another benefit is that helpers receive training in cooperative techniques and interpersonal skills that will last a lifetime. The program also gives older students a chance to "intern" in the helping professions. Finally, there is the "helping as healing" aspect. As they coach helpees in handling problems with other children and adults, helpers have a chance to work through some of their own problems with other children and adults from an emotionally safe distance. Thus, as they foster the personal growth of others, they foster their own personal growth.

Teachers need all the help they can get. As classrooms become more crowded, teachers are more overworked than ever. They must integrate non-English-speaking students into the mainstream and at the same time deal with an ever-increasing number of students with learning and behavioral problems. All this while challenging the leaders and not ignoring the needs of the average student! Peer helpers can alleviate some of the heavy load. Another benefit to teachers is the innovative way peer helping gets older students to learn. Having them teach a subject is a way to refocus their efforts on math or reading skills. Finally, teachers gain the respect and admiration of peer helpers in their classes because the older students can see for themselves what teachers are up against.

Peer helpers have a unique teaching tool: Because they are close to the age of the helpees, they can talk their language.

3. A Peer Helping Success Story

The concepts, activities and practical suggestions in this book are based upon my experiences organizing and running a peer helping program at Westwood Elementary School in Poway Unified, San Diego, California. Westwood's K-5 population includes 950 middle- to upper-middle-class students.

I first got the idea for a peer helping program after observing the exciting results of the peer counseling program Cathy Moran had organized at Poway High School. As I began to visualize adapting her program to my school, I became possessed with the idea. I was determined to get the program in place for the coming year. In a mad rush I worked day and night designing the model, talking to key people, and making preparations for the implementation of the program. I did all this in six weeks.

In truth, I intuitively went through all the processes described in this book, but compressed them into a short span of time. I made my share of mistakes—too many, actually. This book will, I hope, prevent your making the same mistakes and also keep you from "reinventing the wheel" as you develop your program in a logical, step-by-step fashion.

The first year, I had twenty-five peer helpers tutoring after school for a half hour and mentoring social skills twice a week for twenty minutes during recess. Thus, peer helpers "worked" (though they don't consider it work) a little more than one hour a week. The next year, the program doubled to include fifty peer helpers, but this time they tutored during their lunch periods. I found this to be a more satisfactory arrangement. Of the fifty who tutored, twenty-five also mentored social skills during helpees' recesses. The program still follows this same structure, only now we have a special "Games" program whereby peer helpers lead groups of younger children in games like jacks and Parcheesi. Because I use my own classroom as the meeting place for peer helpers, the program is capped at fifty helpers.

A formal evaluation was conducted in Spring 1992 by San Diego State University educational technology student Mary Fox. The report happily confirmed the success of the program's first year. Here are a few highlights:

- 45% of teachers and 48% of parents reported a large improvement in their students' ability to get along with other children.

- 36% of teachers and 38% of parents perceived a large to very large improvement in their students' academic skills.

- 73% of teachers and 76% of parents perceived a significant improvement in students' self-esteem.

- 82% of teachers and 71% of parents perceived a significant improvement in their students' social skills.

- 94% of parents and teachers wanted the program to continue.

All parties benefit—just as I had hoped. The helpees' parents are enthusiastic about the special relationships they see growing between their child and the peer helper. "The children can't wait for the peer helpers to show up," says one second-grade teacher. "They get so much from each other. Plus, helping has now become an 'in' activity at Westwood."

The big surprise continues to be how much the peer helpers themselves get out of the program. The Student Study Team at our school finds peer helping to be such a growth experience that it now includes referring some "at risk" students to be helped by peer helpers as an intervention.

As the advisor, I've learned a great deal and grown in ways I never thought possible. One of the great "perks" in taking on a big job like this is that you get to work with a group of dedicated, outstanding kids who gradually become your friends and confidantes as you work together over time. For me, the peer helping program forms the core of why I love my job.

Part Two

Planning

If you don't know
where you're going,
you might end up
somewhere else.
—Anonymous

In this section you will work through the following seven steps in preparation for your own peer helping program:

1. Assess your school's needs.

2. Write up goals based on needs.

3. Study the peer helping model in Part Three.

4. Make a proposal.

5. Gain administrative approval.

6. Refine your proposal based on staff and other input.

7. Promote your program.

4. Assessing Your School's Needs

You're reading this book because you think your school has a need for peer helping. You may have received the "go-ahead" from an administrator for initiating such a program. However, before getting started, you need to systematically gather information to tailor your program to fit your school's exact needs. These may not turn out to be the same needs that you perceive them to be at the start. A good front-end analysis can spare you unnecessary surprises and wasted time later on.

If you haven't informally surveyed the staff for their ideas, now is the time. It is important to build staff enthusiasm and interest before you begin. The more input they have in the initial development of the proposal, the more they will support it later. It is also wise to gather opinions in a more formal survey. In what areas will helpees most likely need help? And of course, you need to find out how much time the teachers are willing to put in on the program and how flexible they will be with the logistics. Appendix Form A-1 is a sample Needs Assessment Survey.

Are any parents interested in helping? Meet with the PTA to solicit feedback and support.

After you have gathered opinions from a variety of sources including students and parents, analyze the results to see if a peer helping program is feasible. Ask yourself the following questions:

- What will your role be in the program?
  Can you identify any staff members

A good front-end analysis can spare you unnecessary surprises and wasted time later on.

who seem willing to assist you with the program?

- Can you estimate the number of helpees and helpers that you will have?

- Will you have need of more tutors or mentors?

- What limitations cropped up in the assessment process?

- What seem to be the priorities of administration and staff?

- How will the program relate to other school activities?

- Do teachers and administrators strongly support the program? If not, what objections do they have? Are there ways you can design your program to get around these objections?

- Are there any school policies that will make implementation of the program difficult?

- By what date must the program be ready for use?

- What funds will be available for planning and development?

- What personnel will be available?

- What about a meeting place for helpers?

By answering these questions up front, you can customize your program to take any priorities or constraints into account. By presenting a more realistic proposal to the administration, you increase your chances for approval.

By presenting a more realistic proposal to the administration, you increase your chances for approval.

5. Writing Up Goals

Now you need to write out some general goals to help you focus on what you are trying to accomplish with your program. These clearly stated goals will help you make decisions as you customize the program for your school; later these goals will help you evaluate your program. Much later on, you will assist helpers in writing up specific objectives for their work with helpees.

If you are setting up a program that includes both tutors and mentors, you will find that they share many of the same goals. However, I think it's easier to draw up two separate lists. Here are some possibilities:

Goals for a Peer Tutoring Program

- Provide individualized instruction

- Help students improve their grades

- Offer fun and creative ways to learn

- Help students develop a more positive attitude toward school

- Increase students' self-esteem

- Provide positive role models for students

- Help build relationships across age and ethnic groups

- Improve attendance

Clearly stated goals will help you make decisions as you customize the program for your school.

Goals for a Peer Mentoring Program

- Increase students' self-esteem

- Help build relationships across age and ethnic groups

- Role-model cooperative techniques and interpersonal skills

- Provide positive role-models for students

- Help students make friends

- Help integrate isolated individuals into a group

- Help reduce classroom disruptions through conflict-resolving skills

- Reduce playground "incidents"

- Reduce littering and property destruction

6. Studying the Model

Your next step is to familiarize yourself with the various components of a peer helping program and the options for each component as presented in Part Three. Read it carefully and try to relate the model to the unique needs of your school.

7. Making a Proposal

Based on what you know at this point, make tentative decisions for all of the elements within the model. Make sure you have taken into consideration and allowed for the input of administrators and staff. Explore all the alternatives before deciding on the best one. Here is a checklist of elements that you should include in your proposal:

Proposal Checklist

☐ Meeting Place

☐ Peer Helper Meeting Times (weekly, bi-weekly, monthly)

☐ Structure of Tutoring Program (before/after school or during school

☐ Structure of Mentoring Program

☐ Recruitment Procedure

☐ Organization and Development of Training Program

☐ Procedure for Obtaining Referrals

☐ Procedures for Matching Peer Helpers with Helpees and/or Teachers

☐ Responsibilities of Peer Helping Team Members

☐ Personnel

☐ Budget

☐ Timeline

🍎

Make sure you have taken into consideration and allowed for the input of administrators and staff.

8. Gaining Administrative Approval

When you make your formal proposal presentation to the appropriate administrator, be professional. Make sure your pitch is carefully thought out. Include what the program will do for the students and what the administration and staff will gain from it. Be prepared to discuss both financial and personnel needs. Your enthusiasm and positive attitude are vital in gaining approval and support.

Include what the program will do for the students and what the administration and staff will gain from it.

9. Refining Your Proposal

Listen carefully to the feedback you receive and, based on this, finalize your program. Be flexible. Remember, you're going to need the cooperation of everyone on the staff if the program is going to work, so now is the time to let them know how easy it is to work with you! Also, if you've done a good job communicating with staff members and have provided them with adequate opportunity to explore ideas with you and get information from you, they will tell others about your program and help you with public relations, fundraising, and removing other roadblocks along the way.

Be flexible.

10. Promoting Your Program

Your plan may look good on paper, but if you don't talk it up and develop a base of support, the most brilliant plan may fall flat. Make presentations to parents groups, get the word out in a newsletter, submit an article to the local newspaper. A strong support base means more resources may materialize. Part Four offers more tips about public relations.

If you don't talk it up and develop a base of support, the most brilliant plan may fall flat.

Part Three

Customizing the Model

Write your plans in pencil, and always carry a big eraser.
— Anonymous

This section presents a model of a peer helping program, detailing the options for basic elements that need to be included. Peer helping programs are not "one size fits all." The options offered in this model are by no means exhaustive; therefore, pick and choose those items that work for you and seek new and creative alternatives for the rest.

Peer helping programs are not "one size fits all."

11. Choosing a Meeting Place

A private peer helper workroom with a carpeted floor and movable chairs and walls covered with peer helping-related paraphernalia—in other words, a peer helping headquarters—would be the dream choice. Here peer helpers could unwind and process their tutoring or mentoring sessions. They could get recharged after the sometimes draining business of helping others.

However, if this is unrealistic, a cozy corner of a classroom or guidance/administrative office could also work. It is important that the helpers have a place where they can find you and leave messages for other helpers. A bulletin board where they can display posters, pictures, progress charts, photographs, and work done by helpees is ideal.

It is important that the helpers have a place where they can find you and leave messages for other helpers.

12. Scheduling Meeting Times

Possibilities include meeting every other week during regularly scheduled class time, during the lunch period, or before or after school. I recommend that the bulk of initial training meetings (ten to fifteen hours) be held over a weekend. If this won't work, then some combination of during- and after-school training hours can be arranged.

Ongoing meetings are used to discuss problems (e.g., what to do about helpees who cling to helpers during free periods) and successes (e.g., how 1st-graders aren't fighting as much as they used to). Ideas for innovative ways to teach a subject are shared. If desired, training in conflict resolution, interpersonal skills, etc., may be carried out at this time. Most importantly, be available for open discussion to meet the needs of the helpers!

13. Developing the Program Structure

During-School Tutoring

Scheduling peer tutoring during the school day works best. It insures greater participation and allows the receiving teacher to supervise the tutoring in the regular classroom. You have two options for scheduling during-school tutoring.

1. Helpers tutor helpees while they are on their lunch break. This involves the least pull-out time for peer helpers.

2. Helpers are excused from their classes once a week to go the helpee's room for a thirty-minute or more tutoring session.

Whichever option you choose, the specific day for tutoring will be decided between the peer helper and the receiving teacher. (I recommend that a peer helper be assigned to a particular teacher for the year. This encourages better communication and also allows the peer helper to work with others in the same classroom. See Chapter 18, "Making a Good Match," for more about this.)

Before- or After-School Tutoring

Scheduling tutoring for before or after school also works well, even though fewer students can participate in the program and rooms and supervision must be arranged. The receiving teacher usually prepares the work for the helpee, who arrives at the tutoring session with assignments in hand. Tutoring takes place in a room designated for this purpose, with an adult supervisor present.

Using the before- or after-school schedule requires that transportation be pre-arranged. Usually K-2 students are picked up by parents at the end of tutoring. Parents of participants in a before-school program must contact the partner if their child is going to be absent.

During-School Mentoring

Interaction for peer mentoring is most desirable on the playground, so mentoring usually takes place during school. Helpers work with their helpees for approximately twenty-five minutes during the helpee's lunch recess. The peer helper is dismissed early from his or her before-lunch class in order to be on the playground with a younger schoolmate, whose lunch is usually earlier.

Within this structure, you have two options for scheduling.

1. Helpers assist helpees with social skills in a one-on-one situation.

2. Helpers set up game stations and lead helpees in group-play situations.

In one-on-one mentoring, a peer helper is matched with a younger student who needs assistance in learning skills such as how to interact with others or how to make friends. Remember, receiving teachers should not assign helpers to students with extreme behavior problems—the goal of the program is to achieve success for both helper and helpee.

In group-play mentoring, helpers set up a game center at a convenient location on the playground. They bring out the games three days a week. All students, not just helpees, are allowed to participate. Several peer helpers "supervise" the games and assist younger students with social skills during the interaction. This option allows all the helpers to get involved, whereas the first option requires only as many helpers as there are helpees.

Once you set up your schedule, it should remain the same throughout the year. See Appendix Forms A-2 and A-3 for detailed tutoring and mentoring schedules. Use these as a starting point as you plan and develop your program's structure.

14. Selecting Peer Helpers

Who makes a good peer helper? The selection criteria are the same for both tutors and mentors. You will probably want to add your own criteria to this suggested list.

A good peer helper is an older student in fourth, fifth, or sixth grade who is:

- interested in helping others

- sensitive to other people

- accepting of others

- responsible

- tolerant of differences

- caring

- flexible

- honest

- energetic

A straight-A academic record is not a prerequisite. Often someone who has experienced frustration in learning makes a more patient teacher. However, it is a good idea to include high achievers, especially as you start your program. Teachers will feel less apprehensive about excusing these students from class to work with their helpees. Also, including one or two students who are well-liked and visible on campus confers instant status on the program in the eyes of their peers.

Selecting your group of peer helpers is one of the most critical steps in the program. You are ultimately accountable for the behavior of your peer helpers, so don't be tempted to make exceptions to the selection criteria you decide on. A peer helping program is no place for students who behave irresponsibly or who require constant supervision.

Recruiting

The first and most preferable option, the open-selection process, is the most involved but also the most democratic. This approach is most likely to turn up outstanding peer helpers who are highly motivated and dedicated. This option encourages students to completely "own" the program from start to finish.

Here are the steps to follow when using an open-selection process:

- Gain support of key teachers who will "prime the pump" for you by talking up the program to generate interest and to convey the idea that peer helping is a high-status activity.

- Make presentations to 4th-, 5th-, and 6th-grade students. I recommend holding separate assemblies for each upper grade so that the sixth-graders won't overshadow the younger ones. Explain the general program, the training sessions, the time commitment, and the criteria for getting into the program. During this presentation, make very clear to the students what your expectation of them will be. Include at least the following points so that students know what their responsibilities will be:

1. Peer helping is a year-long commitment.

The open-selection process is most likely to turn up outstanding peer helpers who are highly motivated and dedicated.

2. Attending the two-day training session is mandatory. If they will not be able to attend, they should not apply.

3. Peer helpers must be available for ongoing training.

   Then briefly explain the application process. Make sure you mention that space is limited; this paves the way for any rejection notices you might have to send out.

- Interested students ask their teachers for an application packet. Application packets include student application, parent permission forms, and teacher recommendations (Appendix Forms A-4 through A-8 comprise the complete packet). Students and parents complete Forms A-4 through A-6. Students must also get a letter of recommendation from an outside adult (not a relative or teacher) to include with their application. Finally, students give their entire packets to their teachers for recommendations. Teachers, in turn, return the whole packet to the peer helping advisor. Allow one week for students to complete and return the packet.

Emphasize to the students that the ability to complete the packet on schedule will be a leading indicator of their suitability for the program. Accomplishing this first task will indicate to you that they have a sense of responsibility and commitment, and that they know how to follow directions. You, too, must follow through on this. In no case should you accept late or incomplete application packets. Such applications should be returned to the student with Form A-9, "Notice of Incomplete or Late Application."

The following two recruiting options are less desirable and should only be used if there are time restraints or other similar, unavoidable circumstances. Once the program is successfully established, you can switch your recruiting efforts over to the open-selection process.

1. Handpick five or six students with whom you would like to work.

2. Ask for recommendations from faculty members and administrators. Have them fill out the recommendation forms (see Forms A-7 and A-8 in the student application packet). You can add their list to your pool of possible recruits. Then make your selection from these.

Interviewing

After you have screened ratings sheets and application forms and eliminated unqualified applicants, you can set up an interview schedule. Before you begin interviewing, review the following suggestions for the process:

- Have teachers notify interviewees of their appointment time the day before the interview is scheduled.

- Have one or two other interviewers work with you. Interviewers can be teachers, instructional aides, or parent volunteers.

- Interview in groups of up to eight students. If possible, schedule all interviews for one day. This means you will need to be freed from your regular responsibilities.

- Schedule ten to fifteen minutes per interview. This is followed by a five- to ten-minute break to assess the interviews. It is important to write down results immediately following the interview.

- Keep groups homogeneous. That is, do not mix 4th-, 5th-, and 6th-graders together at this time. If possible, keep students from the same class in the same group. This helps the students feel more relaxed and open in their discussion.

See Appendix Forms A-10 and A-11 for a sample interview agenda and scoring sheet.

Final Selection

Remember that the interview is just one aspect of the application procedure; some potentially great peer helpers may just not interview well. Don't be afraid to use your instincts. Also, realize that it is relatively easy to turn a student down at this point. Later, after you've worked together trying to improve interpersonal skills and it's still not working out, it's very painful to ask someone to leave.

Notification of Acceptance or Rejection

Call a short meeting after school or during lunch to pass out the letters. Make sure you offer to talk privately to those who were not selected. See Appendix Forms A-12 and A-13 for sample acceptance/rejection notices. Note that Form A-12, "Notice of Acceptance," also requires that parents/guardians give permission for their children to attend the peer helper training.

15. Scheduling the Orientation Meeting

After the peer helpers have been selected, organize a meeting for them and their parents. This meeting should take place at least two to three days prior to the training session. At the meeting, introduce yourself and other involved personnel to the parents, explain the purpose of the program, and answer questions. Then ask for their support. Let them know about the time commitment involved. If some parents decide against their child participating in the program, you still have time to recruit a replacement.

16. Training the Peer Helpers

The most critical phase of your program is the training of the peer helpers. Effective training often makes the difference between a successful program and an unsuccessful one. The content of training will vary from group to group because each group has different needs. Use the training activities and formats presented in this book as a starting point. You may also want to add activities of your own.

Developing Goals

Writing training goals will help you develop the curriculum for training. Regardless of the scope of your program, your goals will probably include the following:

- To build on the students' own natural helping behavior

- To develop mutual trust and group cohesiveness

- To develop self-awareness

- To make students aware of the need for helping skills

- To model and practice the desired helping skills

- To receive feedback on communication skills

- To learn a code of ethics

> The most critical phase of your program is the training of the peer helpers.

- To become familiar with program procedures

- To learn a basic model of human behavior

- To be aware of the pitfalls of the program

The training activities and discussion topics will relate directly to these goals. This book offers complete activities and discussion guides for the initial training session and offers resources for material to be used in ongoing training.

Setting the Tone

The trainer and/or advisor set the tone for the program. It is important that an atmosphere of warm acceptance be established at the start. The trainer must model the high-level helping skills, ethical behavior, and friendly concern that you want your helpers to model.

Choosing the Method of Training

The initial peer helper training ideally takes place over two days. Training is scheduled on a Friday after school from 4 to 8 P.M. and from 9 A.M. to 5 P.M. the next day. A marathon training session like this one is a great way for everyone to get to know each other and become familiar with the program. The fun activities are aimed at building group cohesiveness, trust, self-awareness, and communication skills while familiarizing helpers with responsibilities and procedures of the peer helping program.

A sample agenda for the two-day training model is on the following page.

The trainer must model the high-level helping skills, ethical behavior and friendly concern that you want your helpers to model.

TWO-DAY TRAINING AGENDA

Friday

3:15 - 4:00 P.M.	Staff Meeting; Set Up Room
4:00 - 5:15	Introduction; Signature Hunt; Who Am I?; Name Tags; Rules for Training
5:15 - 6:00	Dinner Triads; Sharing Self
6:00 - 6:15	Introductions
6:15 - 6:45	Me Shield
6:45 - 7:00	Discussion: Reason for Peer Helping; Rules for Peer Helpers
7:00 - 7:15	Let Go and Trust
7:15 - 7:45	Poster Activity; Share Posters
7:45 - 8:00	Self-Assessment — "I" Statements
8:00	Parents Pick Up Students

Saturday

8:30 - 9:00 A.M.	Staff Meeting
9:00 - 9:15	Triads; Review Learning from Friday
9:15 - 9:45	We're Sticking Together
9:45 - 10:30	IALAC Skit and Posters
10:30 - 10:45	Break
10:45 - 11:00	Who Am I?
11:00 - 11:30	Discussion: How to Tutor/How to Mentor
11:30 - 12:15 P.M.	Lunch with Two New People
12:15 - 12:30	Let Go and Trust
12:30 - 1:00	Remember the Time
1:00 - 1:30	Discussion: Social Skills
1:30 - 2:00	Skits
2:00 - 2:15	Break
2:15 - 2:45	I Am Special
2:45 - 3:15	Letter to Self
3:15 - 3:45	Discussion: Peer Helping Procedures
3:45 - 4:00	Numbers in Order
4:00 - 4:20	Skit Practice
4:20 - 4:45	Certificates, Question & Answers, Cleanup
4:45 - 5:00	Parents Arrive; Self-Assessment "I" Statements; Present Skits; Dismiss
5:00 - 5:30	Staff Meeting

A detailed, expanded agenda and preparation checklist for the training session are in Appendix B, Forms B-1 through B-4. Forms B-5 through B-11 comprise the training packet all students receive, including: "Do's and Don'ts for Peer Helpers"; "How to Tutor/ How to Mentor"; "Peer Helper's Code of Ethics"; log sheet/record of activities; and training evaluation.

A second training option is the after-school schedule. If you have to hold your initial training during after-school hours, divide the two-day agenda into three- or four-day sessions.

Follow-Up Training Meetings

It is impossible for you to cover all the necessary peer helping topics in the initial training session; follow-up training is essential. Reinforcing the skills learned in initial training and introducing new skills are necessary to keep the program exciting. This follow-up training usually takes place at the peer helper meetings.

Possible topics for discussion in the regular follow-up meetings should include creative and fun ways to teach different subjects, such as:

- principles of human behavior

- role-playing

- role reversals

- advanced interpersonal skills

- problem-solving and conflict resolution

- communication stoppers

- stress management

- motivation of students

- and of course, anything you didn't cover in the initial training.

The Resources section at the back of this book lists several books that deal exclusively with training activities.

Follow-up training is essential.

17. Identifying Receiving Teachers

After teachers attend the faculty meeting, wherein the peer helping program is officially introduced, distribute a "Teacher Request for Peer Helpers" (Appendix Form A-14).

18. Making a Good Match

Careful consideration must be taken when matching a peer helper with a helpee or receiving teacher. Depending upon the particular program structure you choose (see Chapter 13), there are some options for making a match.

During-School Tutoring

If you schedule peer tutoring for during school, you will match a helper to a specific classroom teacher with whom the helper will work throughout the year. This helper will then work with any student in that classroom in need of academic assistance. The larger the program, the more helpers you will be able to assign each teacher. Two to three peer helpers to a receiving teacher are plenty.

Before- or After-School Tutoring

If you schedule peer tutoring for before or after school, you will match a helper with a particular helpee. If you choose this option, exercise great care when creating a match, as the experience will have a significant impact for both students.

One-on-One Mentoring

If you choose this option instead of the game-center option, you will be assigning one helper to one helpee. Pay close attention to the needs of the helpee, and get frequent feedback from the receiving teacher. Try to match a boy with a boy and a girl with a girl whenever possible. Avoid matching shy helpers with helpees who have trouble making friends.

Guidelines for Matching

- If a peer helper asks to work with a specific receiving teacher, try to honor that request. Usually a bond between the two already exists, and their working relationship will form quickly and smoothly.

- When assigning a peer helper to a classroom or individual helpee, it is best to establish a two-year difference between the grade levels. This will set up a more respectful peer relationship, and each student's role will be clearly defined.

- The more students have in common, the better. If the applications and teacher request forms identify helpers and helpees with areas of common interest, match them up.

19. Defining the Responsibilities of Receiving Teachers

Remember, the receiving teacher is the one who has requested a peer helper to tutor or mentor their students. This person has four main responsibilities.

To Build Up the Helper

Besides referring helpees for the program, the receiving teacher's role is a key one to the success of the program. Receiving teachers should praise peer helpers at every opportunity, letting them know they are valued partners in teaching their students. As such, teachers should meet frequently with helpers to share opinions and ask for suggestions and ideas. The receiving teacher may even include the helper in part of the parent conference. It is this aspect of the program that keeps the peer helpers happy and prevents burn-out.

To Make Sure the Helper Understands the Task

Receiving teachers give clear directions and check to see if they're understood. Telling the helper the goal of an assignment and why it's important helps direct his or her efforts. Receiving teachers must give helpers important jobs to do, not "flunky" work like cleaning up after an art project or babysitting an unruly student.

To Supervise

Despite clear instructions, the helper may still miss the point of an assignment and go off on a tangent. Receiving teachers need to provide occasional over-the-shoulder supervision to get things back on track. It is surprising how unhelpful peer helpers can be when they have forgotten their training and start acting out their own imaginative concepts of being "teachers."

To Keep Interested People Informed

The receiving teacher should let parents, the advisor, and the sending teacher know how the sessions are going. If a problem occurs during a session, it should be reported immediately to the peer helping advisor. Again, communication is a key factor in the success of this program.

20. Defining the Responsibilities of Sending Teachers

The primary responsibility of the sending teacher is to support the peer helper. Successful sending teachers let peer helpers know they are making a valuable contribution. They show their support by being cooperative about scheduling issues, and they realize missed class time does not mean a student is cutting their class in order to goof off. They appreciate the fact that helpers are gaining human relations skills and making their own academic work more meaningful.

Part Four

Managing a Successful Program

Success is a journey,
not a destination.
— Ben Sweetland

We have now worked through most of the peer helping model, covering items from which you will choose when you draw up your proposal. The topics covered in this section present ideas for gaining support from colleagues and parents and ensuring the success of your program.

The road to a successful peer helping program is of necessity a winding one. Frequent circling back to check the progress you hope you've made, making detours to the jungle gym and learning center, taking sidetrips to the copy machine, and meeting temporary dead-ends before a mountain of paperwork are all part of the scenery. If you take the shortcut you'll get there faster, but you may miss critical steps. The long way is the only way if you want a successful and enduring program.

21. Recruiting Personnel

As the advisor you play many roles. You are instructional designer, organizer, trainer, facilitator, counselor, evaluator, media specialist, public relations writer, administrator, secretary, politician, public speaker, supervisor, manager, community liaison, friend, confidante, and role-model. You do all this while exhibiting advanced interpersonal skills, a profound dedication to children, and unbridled enthusiasm for your job!

If this sounds more like a job for Superman than for a single human being with the normal range of skills and hours in the day in which to use them, you're right. That's why it is essential for you to get some help. If your program is small—less than ten helpers—you can probably do it all. But if it's bigger, see if you can find one or two other people to help you share the load. A co-advisor arrangement works well at some schools. At the very least, you will need to recruit additional help for the initial training session. Now is the time to take stock of your own skills. If you find, for example, that you are an excellent organizer and can get the program up and running in no time, but that under extreme pressure, your interpersonal skills resemble Attila the Hun's, you should enlist the help of a trainer. This person can make up for your weak areas while you work on improving these skills within yourself.

Some peer helping advisors have found it helpful to ask another staff member to act as co-advisor. A partner can help you with the formidable logistics of the program as well as provide you with a support system when you need it.

22. Communicating: The Key to Success

Peer helping is a communications game and you're the head coach. This diagram shows a model of your peer helping team.

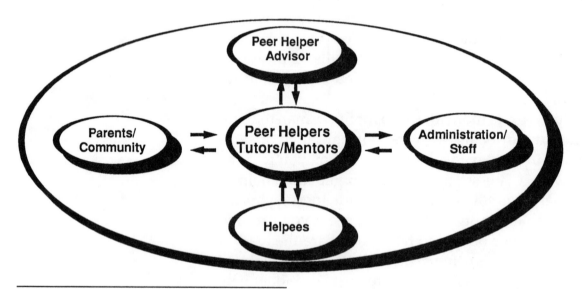

Peer Helping Team Communications Model

Note that the peer helpers stand at the center. As the central focus of the program, their communication with other members of the team is built in as part of the program. They are scheduled to meet with helpees and teachers and with you as part of the ongoing training meetings.

On the other hand, you, the coach, are positioned at the top and not directly linked to everyone else on the loop. What does this mean for you? It means that those communication lines along the perimeter of the model must be generated by you. The structure of the program itself does not automatically guarantee interaction between you and the helpees, parents, teachers, administrators, and members of the community. You must take the initiative to set up and maintain these lines of communication. Breakdowns in communication are a common cause of a failed program.

Communicate with Peer Helpers on a Regular Basis

Yes, you will be meeting with them regularly, but be available in between for help. For example, a day or two before they are to meet with their helpees for the first time, schedule a quick meeting to affirm their skills; a discussion of how they get to the room and what exactly they plan to do with the helpee will reduce their initial anxiety. Then meet with them a couple of times during their first few sessions. You constantly need to be setting expectations, praising, giving feedback, listening, informing them of schedule changes, reminding them of meeting times, teaching new skills, and sharing ideas.

Coordinate with Staff and Administration

Too often, a new program like this one is treated as if it occupies a special world of its own. The special privileges that peer helpers receive in terms of time out of regular class and a special room may irritate staff and administration unless they are fully informed about the program. Also, administrators and teachers typically don't like surprises. Make sure to coordinate and communicate any changes in scheduling and inform them of any events that may interest them professionally. Developing understanding and respect for you and the program will reduce resentment that might be building up.

Breakdowns in communication are a common cause of a failed program.

Make a Point to Seek Out Helpees

You will hear indirectly how things are going, but it never hurts to get out there and see for yourself. It's a natural tendency to shield the "boss" from bad news; therefore, it's not always wise to assume that things are going exactly as stated.

Communicate Regularly with Parents

Have a file of form letters to send to keep parents informed. These should include the initial letter to parents explaining the program (Form A-5) and follow-through letters to let them know how the peer helpers and helpees are doing. If you have a before- or after-school program, set up a phone system so that parents and students can rearrange transportation if a helper or helpee is absent.

Promote Your Program to the Community

Here are some ideas for your public relations department:

- Write articles for the school newsletter and for the local newspaper any time the peer helpers take on an interesting project. The beginning of the program and the end-of-the-year recognition ceremony are ideal.

- You and a panel of peer helpers can make group presentations to local civic organizations such as the Rotary, Chamber of Commerce, the PTA, or Kiwanis.

- Order peer helping T-shirts for advertising and team-building purposes. Use the "PEERS" logo found on the appendices pages if you wish.

- Make professional presentations to teachers' groups.

- Join the National Peer Helpers Association, which was founded in 1987, and subscribe and submit articles to the *Peer Facilitator's Quarterly*. The address is P.O. Box 2684, Greenville, NC 27834.

- Attend a Peer Helpers Conference with your students. They'll have fun and you'll have something else to write about.

23. Supervising: "MBWA"

We've just covered the most vital element involved in supervising a program: getting out there and communicating. Tom Peters, the business writer and columnist, calls this style of management "MBWA," or Management By Walking Around. Tutors and mentors are only human; knowing that their skills are being monitored, they will use the top-flight interpersonal skills they have learned in training.

Everybody is a supervisor. Receiving teachers perform the bulk of the hands-on supervision (see Chapter 19 to review the responsibilities of the receiving teacher). They need to do periodic over-the-shoulder checks to see if peer helpers are effectively tutoring and/or mentoring their students. Sending teachers must be there to provide guidance and support to peer helpers. Advisors provide direction for the entire program, personally dropping in on the classroom and the playground to carefully observe the interaction that takes place.

24. Conducting Evaluations

Systematic evaluations are necessary to develop and maintain a quality program. Evaluations let you know what's working and what's not. The following questions are answered by various types of evaluations:

- Was the training effective?

- What were the weak spots?

- What do the peer helpers really think about the program and about you as the advisor?

- Is the program meeting its goals?

- Is mentoring having an impact on the behavior of the helpees?

- Is tutoring leading to better grades?

- What could you improve next year?

Evaluating the Progress of the Helpee

The focal point of your program is the improvement that takes place in the interaction between the helpee and the tutor or mentor. Direct observation of this interaction is the best way to evaluate the progress of a mentoring situation. The receiving teacher and peer helper write down comments and descriptions of behaviors in anecdotal form. You should also obtain feedback from parents. Accumulated data of this sort over time provides a valuable evaluation of the learning process.

This same method is applied to tutoring. Such anecdotal information, backed up by grades and standardized test scores, provides a solid basis for evaluating the progress of the tutoring.

Evaluating the Program

Program evaluation can accomplished in a variety of ways, as outlined below. Numbers 1 and 2 are an integral part of the peer helping program; they incorporate formal surveys that will provide the most in-depth feedback. Number 3 is strongly recommended to promote occasional, informal feedback from students and staff. Number 4 may also be implemented if you determine a need for it.

1. **Peer-helper training evaluation:** Peer helpers fill out this evaluation to express how effective they think their training was. See Appendix Form B-12.

2. **Peer helping program evaluations:** These are filled out by the peer helpers, teachers and parents at the end of a semester or year to assess their perceptions of the strengths and weaknesses of the overall program. See Appendix Forms C-1, C-2, and C-3.

3. **Verbal reassurance:** As the peer-helping advisor, you should check in with participating students periodically to see how it's going. Check in with teachers on campus as well, just to make sure everything is running smoothly. Sometimes, teachers may be reluctant to come to you, so drop in on them two or three times a year. Or send a memo asking them to share any concerns about (or praises for!) the program.

4. Student Sharing: Peer helpers can write down comments in their own log or in a log kept in the peer helpers' workroom. They can also give feedback at follow-up meetings, which you may choose to record on newsprint or on the board.

25. Keeping Good Records

Set up a filing system that includes not only all forms—applications, evaluations, permission slips, rating sheets, calendars, schedules, and sample letters—but also a folder of successful ideas and new ones that you might develop. A file folder with pertinent quotes, research findings and other articles relevant to peer helping will come in handy when you're preparing a presentation. You might start with this one:

> In our society peer influence may be the strongest single motivational force in a student's life.

This was part of a position statement by the American School Counselor Association in 1978 (revised in 1984).

Keep exact accounts of all purchases, materials, and equipment you check out.

You must keep detailed records of any negative interactions. Remember, you're accountable, so leave a "paper trail."

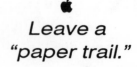

Leave a "paper trail."

26. Using Your Resources

Here are some tips for making the most of your resources:

- Check with the school and district librarians to see if they have materials on interpersonal skills, tutoring, role-modeling or anything related to peer helping.

- The resource room specialist might have good tutoring/computer game materials suitable for your purposes.

- County offices of education often maintain professional libraries complete with masters and doctoral theses, education kits, and other materials you can borrow.

- Develop your own supplementary handouts and forms.

- See if you can obtain funds from the PTA or other sources to purchase peer helping handbooks. This will save you lots of time in the copying room (and the hassle of writing for photocopying permissions).

- Check out media equipment you need regularly: cassette recorders, record player. See if VCRs and cameras for videotaping are available.

- Peer helpers can develop and produce their own teaching materials, such as puppets or math games.

27. Budgeting

There is no such thing as a free peer helping program. If you have no expenses, then your program is either short on substance or you are picking up some costs yourself. Anticipate expenditures so you can include them in your initial proposal. The following are items that might appear on your budget:

- personnel time (trainer aides, clerical support)

- renovation of required facilities

- purchase or preparation of materials

- replacement of damaged materials/equipment

- photocopying costs

- administrative costs (travel, telephone, postage)

- maintenance of equipment

- periodic updating of program materials

- guest speakers

- other special projects

28. Adding New Projects

Your program may get stale, and unchallenged helpers may drop out if you don't introduce new and exciting ideas. Tutoring and mentoring will probably be more than enough for the first year, but returning helpers may want something new. Here are some ideas:

- "Dial-a-Smile" is a structured program that organizes phone calling between peer helpers and latch-key children.

- "Meeters and Greeters" welcome new students who are making the transition to a new school environment.

- ESL discussion groups led by peer helpers assist non-English speaking students with learning survival skills.

- In panels or in skits/role-playing, peer helpers lead whole classroom discussions on topics such as wellness/stress management, drug use, getting along with others, conflict management, child safety, AIDS, and stopping putdowns.

- Peer helpers assist handicapped students.

- Videotape conflict resolution techniques or communication skills.

- Peer helpers organize a poster campaign on related topics.

29. Preparing a Final Report

After you have completed one cycle of the process and have had your peer helping program in place for one year, your next step is to prepare a final summary report. Careful attention should be given to this report because it can influence future support for the program.

First, decide for whom the report is to be prepared—administrators, another supporting agency, government grant funding entity, or whomever. By considering those persons who are to receive the report, emphasis or special attention may be given to certain phases of your peer helping program. Explaining how and where funds have been spent may be of primary interest, or evidence of follow-up benefits may be more valuable than details about the learning activities offered in the training.

Second, decide on the report's format. Should it be on paper, or will it be presented on overhead transparencies to a group? In either case, report your results attractively. Here are some suggestions:

- Give the report an interesting title: "Westmont School Finds Peer Helping to Be a Win-Win Situation" or "Why Helping Is 'In' at Westmont School."

- Summarize highlights. Set them off in bullets (as these suggestions are) on the page so they can be grasped quickly.

- Conclude with making appropriate recommendations for next year.

30. Developing a Timeline

The following page shows a model peer helping program over a two-year timeline. It includes all the elements we have covered so far. Depending on the options you choose for your proposal, you may customize the timeline for your individual program.

Two-Year Peer Helping Program Timeline

Year 1

**September -
March**

Planning
Assess needs.
Conduct informal and formal gathering of information.
Research programs at other schools.
Write goals.
Study peer helping model.

April

Customize the Peer Helping Model to Fit Your School
Make tentative decisions on key elements in model.
Write up a proposal.

May

Gain Approval for Proposal
Present proposal to administration and staff.
Modify model based on input.

June-August

Make Final Preparations for Implementation
Prepare peer helper meeting place.
Set up filing system.
Gather materials.
Prepare forms.

Year 2

September

Implement Peer Helping Program
Introduce program at faculty meeting.
Select peer helpers.
Conduct orientation meeting.

October

Hold Initial Training Session
Obtain referrals.
Match tutors/mentors with teachers/helpees.
Send letter to parents.
Finalize scheduling.
Peer helping sessions begin.

**November -
December**

Follow-Up Activities
Conduct ongoing peer helper meetings.
Supervise.
Communicate with all team members.
Submit article to local newspaper.

January - April

Continue Follow-Up

May

Peer Helper Luncheon and Awards Ceremony
Begin evaluations.
Evaluate progress in tutoring and mentoring.
Make final report with recommendations for next year.

31. Recalling the Secrets of Successful Advisors

Your role as peer helper advisor will be a demanding one as well as a rewarding one. You are about to begin the formal planning process for your school's program, so it may be helpful to review some management tips that will help you develop a successful program.

- Peer helping is a kids-helping-kids program, so don't do everything for them. Facilitate and delegate. Be a manager and a mentor in your own right.

- Work hard.

- Listen.

- Care about the people on your team.

- Work within the schedule as much as possible.

- Communicate, communicate, communicate!

- Keep a steady eye on your ultimate purpose.

- Stick to the plan.

32. Reviewing the Organizational Process

Now that you've learned how to plan, implement, and manage a successful peer helping program, it's a good idea to review the overall process we started with.

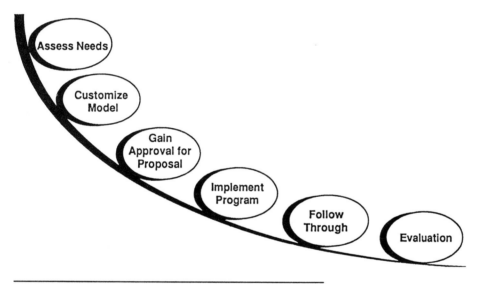

Organizational Process for Peer Helping Program

You are now ready to go back and work through these steps to develop and implement your peer helping program. While you are adding the components, you may find that insights you gain in later planning steps will lead you to revise earlier ones. Therefore, as you go through the sequence, keep your options open.

Building a peer helping program is a complex process that requires keeping many separate elements in mind and continually reevaluating the relationship of each part to the whole. However, it is not so complex that it is too difficult a job for you to take on—remember the peanut butter and jelly analogy!

Part Five

Troubleshooting

We're a team.
If something good
happens, we did it.
If something
outstanding
happens, you did it.
If something
bad happens,
it was my fault.
— Coach Bear
Bryant

A peer helping program is not all sweetness and light and the brotherhood of man. Sometimes bad things happen in spite of doing everything right. The following are the most common peer helping pitfalls and tips for avoiding them.

33. Inadequate Training

First of all, because training demands so much time and preparation, you may be tempted to cut the training phase short. Short encounter groups or one-time workshops or even one-time initial training without followup are inadequate. Poorly trained peer helpers will be less effective in their roles. In the worst case, they may actually do harm. Second, ongoing training is too important to be put on the back burner. Get outside help if you're too bogged down with other aspects of the program.

34. Overemphasis on Helpers' Development

This problem is the opposite of the first. In this scenario, the training program overemphasizes the growth of the peer helpers themselves. Activities developing the peer helpers' self-esteem, self-awareness, and the cohesiveness of the group dominate the training sessions. This happens at the expense of the more fundamental training goal: to apply interpersonal skills *outside* the peer helping group. While a peer helping program does function as a personal support group, this should not be an end in itself. The training and overall focus should reflect the program's ultimate purpose: to enable tutors and mentors to reach out to and support their younger peers.

35. Inadequate Supervision

Instead of "Management By Walking Around" (Chapter 23), advisors lose touch from time to time by barricading themselves in the teacher's lounge or classrooms and sending out the message that they don't want to be disturbed. Understandable as this is, such a situation that needs to be remedied. At least own up to the problem and have a friend sub for you until your other workload subsides.

36. No Evaluation

The lack of an evaluation system is a good predictor of a peer helping program that dies an early death. We've all been schooled in the importance of being accountable for our programs; now we have to follow through. Run off copies of the forms at the back of the book, hand them out, collect them, and you're all set!

37. Lack of Communication

With Administrators

Administrators are paid to worry about risks. They worry about lawsuits resulting from scenarios involving an abusive peer helper or a child getting hurt during a peer helping session. They worry about taxpaying parents who might be angry about their child being taught by a child instead of by a paid professional. They get nervous when you use words like "counseling" when you talk about what a mentor does with his or her helpee on the playground. Some counselors silently seethe when they hear you use this term because they feel it does their profession a disservice, implying that anyone can counsel. Be sensitive to all their concerns.

Gain administrators' confidence and trust by writing up reports of any positive results gleaned from your evaluations, or make a list of positive comments made by parents, teachers, and students. This will reduce anxieties and make them feel that you're really on top of things.

And really be on top of things. Make sure you continue to seek alternative ways for children to relate to children besides with putdowns, threats, and punishments. If you suspect that one of your peer helpers is engaging in negative behavior, suspend his or her helping sessions until you can investigate. If there is an "incident," don't just hope the problem will disappear. Investigate and report the incident to administrators so they can help you with "damage control" measures.

With Staff

Sometimes staff members feel that peer helpers are "taking over the school." Informing staff more about what's going on, plus encouraging peer helpers to maintain a "low profile" in their comings and goings should help.

If a peer helper is in any way a negative force in the classroom, teachers will resent letting him or her miss class. A peer helper who disturbs his or her own classmates certainly doesn't deserve to be in a program which professes to role-model outstanding behavior.

Perhaps you personally are so visible on campus that you arouse resentment in your colleagues for all the attention you are getting. Try thinking about what your program can do for them. Once the program works for them, they'll have to give you their (grudging) support and respect. And last, remember there will always be a certain number of people who will not be pleased no matter what you do!

38. "What Peer Helping Program?"

A dead public relations department means your program dies in the minds of the staff, student body, and community. Try to be visible—without being obnoxious about it. When you have end-of-the-year banquets or other peer helping events, make these moments count. Hit the newspapers and radio. Do a parent mailing. Peer helpers like to work on this sort of thing. A blitz of PR work can harvest big returns in terms of funding, resources, and good will.

39. "Loose lips sink ships"

This old Navy saying is just as true today as it was in World War II. All it takes is one teacher overhearing one peer helper publicly divulging a juicy secret learned from a helpee or one mother learning through the grapevine that her son's peer helper described him as a "brat" to a group of students, and your program is in trouble. You cannot over-emphasize the importance of confidentiality in your training and in your ongoing meetings. Do what the Navy did: Post "Loose lips sink ships" or variations on that theme everywhere you can think of to remind helpers to respect the trust that is given to them.

You cannot overemphasize the importance of confidentiality in your training and in your ongoing meetings.

40. Peer Helper Burn-out

Peer helpers need recharging from time to time. Build plenty of rewards into the structure of your program. Keep a list of possible fun activities just for them, like special holiday parties or other events.

Make sure the receiving teachers understand the need to treat peer helpers as colleagues and to not exploit them by giving them dirty work to perform. Help the receiving teachers be sensitive to the fact that peer helpers get tired of being so helpful, get tired of having their helpees cling to them during recess, and might prefer spending some free time with their own friends.

41. Advisor Burn-out

Sometimes the kindest and most energetic of advisors starts to feel more like a parole officer than a mentor to the mentors. You may feel overworked, unappreciated, and underloved. This is the time to seek out the company and comfort of your own peers. Also, spend some peaceful time alone so that you to can "fill up" after so much giving of skills and love.

Reflect on these words which contain the essential spirit of a peer helping program, the program that your efforts are making possible:

> I expect to pass through life but once. If
> therefore, there be any kindness I can show
> or any good I can do to any fellow being, let
> me do it now, and not defer or neglect it, as I
> shall not pass this way again.
> — William Penn (1644-1718)

Appendix A

Forms for Planning and Initiating Your Peer Helping Program

Form A-1

Needs Assessment Survey

To: Teachers, counselors, administrators

From: (*Your Name Here*)

I am gathering information to assess the need for a peer helping program at our school. The program would provide tutors to help younger students in academic areas and mentors to help students develop social skills. Please fill out this survey and return it to me by (*Date Here*).

Your Name: _____

I. If you work with grades K-4 children, fill out this section.

1. Do you have students who could benefit from academic tutoring? (Circle one.) Yes   No

    If yes, how many? _____

2. In what subjects do your students need help?

3. Could tutoring take place in your room during regular class? Yes   No

4. Would you be willing to supervise tutoring in your classroom before or after school? Yes   No

    Before? Yes   No   After? Yes   No

5. Are you willing to work closely with a peer helper in deciding on and evaluating learning activities? Yes   No

6. Do you have students who could benefit from a mentor who would foster the development of social skills? Yes   No

    If yes, how many? _____

7. Would you be willing to work closely with the mentor in guiding and monitoring the interaction between the mentor and your student? Yes   No

8. Are you interested in being involved with the peer helping program as a:

    Co-advisor? Yes   No

    Advisory board member? Yes   No

    Trainer? Yes   No

    Other?_____

9. Please write additional comments on the reverse.

PEERS II. If you work with grades 4-6 students, fill out this section.

1. Do you have students who would benefit from becoming peer helpers? (Circle one.) Yes   No

   If yes, how many? _____

2. Would you be willing to let these students miss up to an hour of class per week to serve as peer helpers? Yes No

3. Are you willing to support the program in terms of working with the schedule? Yes No

4. Are you interested in being involved with the peer helping program as a:

   Co-advisor? Yes No

   Advisory board member? Yes No

   Trainer? Yes No

   Other?_____

5. Please write additional comments below.

Tutoring and Mentoring

Form A-2

During-School Tutoring Schedule

In this structure, peer helpers tutor once a week in the same classroom all year. As one helpee exits the program, the receiving teacher matches the peer helper with a new one. The receiving teacher and the peer helper decide which day is best. Because we try to keep student pull-out time to a minimum, tutoring occurs during the lunch recess of the peer helper.

Sample School Lunch Schedule

P.M. kindergarten begins at noon.

1st grade	11:00 - 11:45
2nd grade	11:15 - noon
3rd grade	11:30 - 12:15
4th grade	11:45 - 12:30
5th grade	12:00 - 12:45

- 4th graders can tutor in a 1st- or 2nd-grade classroom or in the P.M. kindergarten from noon to 12:30.

- 5th graders can tutor 1st-, 2nd-, and 3rd-grade classes and P.M. kindergarten from 12:15 to 12:45.

- If a 5th-grader tutors a 4th-grader, the 5th-grade peer helper misses the first 15 minutes of class after lunch recess because of overlapping lunch schedules.

- A.M. kindergarten students are tutored by 4th- or 5th-grade students during their 10:30 to 10:45 recess and during the first 15 minutes of class following recess.

During-Lunch Mentoring Schedule

This schedule is based on the lunch schedule of the helpees; therefore, the peer helpers will have to adjust their lunch schedules accordingly.

Sample School Lunch Schedule

1st-grade lunch 11:00 - 11:45   Mentoring from 11:25 - 11:45

2nd-grade lunch 11:15 - noon   Mentoring from 11:40 - noon

3rd-grade lunch 11:30 - 12:15   Mentoring from 11:55 - 12:15

4th-grade lunch 11:45 - 12:30   Mentoring from 12:10 - 12:30

- If a 4th-grade peer helper is mentoring a 1st-grader, he/she will leave class at 11:25—20 minutes earlier than the 4th-grade lunch time—in order to meet with the helpee on the playground. The peer helper mentors for 20 minutes, then eats lunch at the regular time.

- If working with a 2nd-grader, the peer helper leaves class 5 minutes early to mentor, then eats lunch at noon instead of 11:45, followed by a shortened recess.

- If tutoring a 3rd-grader, the peer helper is dismissed for lunch 5 minutes early, eats for 15 minutes, mentors for 20 minutes, then plays for a short time.

- The 5th-grade peer helper's schedule must adjust in a similar fashion.

Sample Game Center Schedule

1st-grade lunch   Games out by 11:20 with 3 to 4 peer mentors

2nd-grade lunch   3 to 4 different mentors out by 11:40

3rd-grade lunch   3 to 4 different mentors out by noon

4th- and 5th-grade lunch   3-4 different mentors out by 12:20

- Games are kept on a cart and are brought out to the designated area by the first group of peer mentors.

- The cart remains out until the end of the last lunch period and is returned by the last group of mentors on duty.

- Monday, Wednesday, and Friday are game days. Fifty peer helpers can cover all these times. If your program is smaller, decrease the number of game days.

Tutoring and Mentoring

Peer Helper Application

Thank you for your interest in becoming a peer helper. The application process consists of five steps, which you must follow precisely to be considered for an interview.

1. Fill out the following questionnaire completely. Do not leave any blanks.

Name _____ Phone _____

Address _____ Date of Birth _____

Teacher _____ Grade _____

1a. Have you had any experiences that would help make you a good peer helper? (List experiences such as babysitting, helping little brothers and/or sisters, being a member of safety patrol, participating in play activities.)

1b. What chores do you do at home?

1c. Name one thing you have done that you are proud of. What makes you proud about this?

1d. When someone makes you angry, what do you do?

1e. What do you think a peer helper does?

PEERS 1f. Why do you think you will make a good peer helper?

2. Carefully read the following commitment statement and sign below.

I understand the responsibilities and time requirements for the peer helper program at our school. I realize that I am committing myself to:

- The initial two-day training session on Friday, *(Date Here)*, from 4 to 8 P.M., and Saturday, *(Date Here)*, from 9 A.M. to 5 P.M.
- Spending one to two lunch recesses a week in a classroom to tutor other students.
- Spending twenty minutes, twice a week, helping students with social skills.
- Attending training meetings two times a month during lunchtime recess.

I understand my responsibility to respect others and follow the ethics on confidentiality

Applicant Signature _____ Date _____

Home phone number _____

3. Your next step is to get a letter of recommendation from an adult who knows you. This letter can be from someone such as a coach, neighbor, family friend, scout leader, etc. The letter may not be from a parent, grandparent, other relative, or any of the teachers at your school. Include the letter in your application packet before turning it in to your teacher.

4. The fourth step is to ask your parent's or guardian's permission to become a peer helper. Explain the program as completely as possible, recalling what you learned from the presentation to your class. Then show your parent/guardian the enclosed cover letter, and ask them to sign the attached form.

5. Once you and your parent/guardian have completed your parts of the application, your final step is to ask your teacher for a letter of recommendation. Give your entire packet to your teacher, and ask him or her to read the cover letter and complete the attached form. Remind your teacher that the completed packet must be turned in to the Peer Helper Advisor by *(Date Here)*.

_____

PEER HELPER ADVISOR USE ONLY: Application received _____

_____

Tutoring and Mentoring

Cover Letter to Parent/Guardian

Dear Parents,

Your child has expressed an interest in becoming a peer helper at school. This program is designed to train older students to assist younger ones in certain areas:

- Peer mentors role-model social skills to students who need help learning to get along better with others. Mentoring occurs during lunchtime recess.

- Peer tutors assist those students who need additional help or enrichment with academics. Tutors are assigned to a classroom and will work closely with the teacher and students in that room all year. Tutors serve one to two days a week for twenty minutes during their lunchtime.

Pullout time from your child's curriculum will be held to a minimum!

If your child has your permission to proceed with the application process, please fill out the attached Parent/Guardian Permission Form. Your child is responsible for completing the Peer Helper Application, getting a letter of recommendation from another adult (non-relative or -teacher), and asking his or her teacher to complete the Teacher Recommendation. The program has been fully explained to the students; ask your child for more details about the application process. Your child is also responsible for turning in the entire packet to his or her teacher on time.

We will be choosing approximately fifty students from the fourth, fifth, and sixth grades to fill the peer helping positions. After interested students have turned in their completed application packets, we will be conducting interviews during the week of *(Date Here)* to make final selections.

If your child is selected, you and he or she will be invited to attend an orientation meeting on *(Date Here)*. Then your child will attend the mandatory two-day training session on Friday, *Date Here)*, from 4 to 8 P.M., and Saturday, *(Date Here)*, from 9 A.M. to 5 P.M. Continued training is necessary for the success of the program, so peer helpers will attend subsequent training sessions, which will be held twice a week during their lunchtime recess. All training will be held at school.

If you have any questions regarding the program, please call me at school *(Your Number Here)*. Thank you for your support.

Sincerely,

(Your Name Here)
Peer Helper Advisor

 **Form A-6**

Parent/Guardian Permission Form

I have read the Parent/Guardian Cover Letter and my child has explained the responsibilities and time requirements of being a peer helper. I support my child's commitment to this program and give my permission for him or her to serve as a peer helper for the *(School Year Here)* school year.

Child's Name _____

Signature of Parent/Guardian _____ Date _____

Cover Letter to Teacher

To: Faculty

From: (*Your Name Here*), Peer Helper Advisor

Date: (*Date Here*)

Re: Recommendations of Peer Helpers

We are beginning the process of selecting peer helpers for our new and exciting peer helping program. Interested students and their parents have completed their applications and the necessary permission forms. The students' final step is to turn their packets over to their teachers. You are asked to fill out the Teacher Recommendation on the reverse, then return the entire packet to me by *(Date Here)*.

Keep the following criteria in mind when making your decision for each student. A good peer helper is someone who is:

- caring
- sensitive to others
- responsible
- flexible
- honest

Thank you for your cooperation.

 **Form A-8**

Teacher Recommendation

Name of Student _____ Date _____

Your Name _____

Rate the student on the following qualities using this scale:

> 1 = Poor
> 3 = Average
> 5 = Outstanding

1. Responsibility _____

2. Self-confidence _____

3. Ability to listen to and understand others _____

4. Enthusiasm _____

5. Maturity _____

6. Flexibility _____

7. Honesty _____

8. Ability to keep confidentiality _____

My overall recommendation is (Circle one):

> 1 - I strongly recommend.
> 2 - I recommend.
> 3 - I recommend with reservations.
> 4 - I do not recommend.

Additional Comments:

The South East Essex
College of Arts & Technology
Carnarvon Road   Southend on Sea   Essex   SS2 6LS
Tel: Southend (0702) 220400   Fax: Southend (0702) 432320

Notice of Incomplete or Late Application

Dear _____ ,

Thank you for applying for the position of peer helper. However, I am returning your application to you for the following reason:

_____ Incomplete application

_____ Parent/Guardian Permission Form not turned in

_____ Letter of recommendation from other adult not turned in

_____ Teacher Recommendation not turned in

_____ Late application

Because your application was not completed properly, I regret to tell you that you lose your chance to be considered for peer helping. I hope you will consider this to be a learning opportunity so that if in the future you are applying for something, you will follow directions carefully.

If you would like to speak with me regarding this, please come to see me in (*Your Room Number*).

Sincerely,

(*Your Name Here*)
Peer Helper Advisor

Interview Agenda

1. Greet interviewees at the door and give them a nametag.

2. Seat the group of 7 to 10 around a table or in a circle of chairs. Because the interview process is set up like a discussion group, students need to be close to each other. Interviewers should sit outside the circle, separate from each other.

3. Introduce the panel of interviewers. Explain that they will be given several questions to answer. The last two will be discussed by the group. Emphasize that there are no right or wrong answers to these questions. They are to brainstorm with the others to discuss their different answers. Make sure they know how a group discussion is carried on.

4. Write the three questions on a chalkboard or flipchart so students can refer to them.
   - **Question 1:** Introduce yourself by giving your name and telling everyone one thing you think is special about you.
   - **Question 2 (Group Brainstorm):** You are a peer helper working with a student who is having trouble doing some math problems the teacher has just introduced in class. What can you do to help him with the work?
   - **Question 3 (Group Brainstorm):** You are mentoring a younger student on the playground. She is having trouble playing by the rules. When playing games, she insists the other kids are cheating her of points, so she quits the game in anger. What can you do?

5. Answering these questions should take no longer than fifteen minutes. Don't go into overtime or you'll lose the opportunity to review each group between interviews. Keep control of the time by thanking interviewees as they complete each answer and move on to the next one.

6. As students are answering the questions, interviewers should sit back, listen attentively, and, after getting a feel for the interviewees, mark on the scoring sheets. Each interviewer should already have these sheets before the interviews begin. The students' names should already be filled in at the top.

7. At the end of the interview session, reassure students of the nice job they did. Tell them when selection results will be available.

8. After each interview session, the interviewers complete the score sheets and add up the totals. This is when the interviewers discuss the candidates. Often, two interviewers will have conflicting assessments of a candidate. If you find a large scoring discrepancy, discuss it. This should only take five to ten minutes.

PEERS

Interview Score Sheet

Date _____

Rate the interviewees on the following qualities, using this scale:

1 = Poor
3 = Average
5 = Outstanding

Student's Name	Grade	Self-Confidence	Group Participation	Listening Skills	Maturity	Enthusiasm	Total

Tutoring and Mentoring

PEERS

Notice of Acceptance

(*Date Here*)

Dear _____ ,

Congratulations on being selected to be a peer helper at our school! All of our peer helpers are well-qualified. I am looking forward to working with all of you this year.

There will be an informal orientation meeting for peer helpers and their parents on (*Date Here*) at (*Time Here*) in the (*Meeting Place Here*). Please plan to attend this meeting, and invite your parents, too. We will discuss the program in more detail at that time.

In addition, mark your calendars now for the training sessions to be held on Friday, (*Date Here*), from 4:00 to 8:00 P.M. and Saturday, (*Date Here*), from 9:00 A.M. to 5:00 P.M.

Once again, congratulations!

Sincerely,

(*Your Name Here*)
Peer Helper Advisor

_____

Please fill out and return to (*Your Name Here*) by (*Date Here*).

_____ Yes, I will be attending the informal meeting. I will be bringing _____ people.

_____ No, I will not be able to attend.

Signature of Peer Helper _____

_____ has my permission to attend the two-day peer helper training session to be held at school on Friday, (*Date Here*), from 4 to 8 P.M. and Saturday, (*Date Here*), from 9 A.M. to 5 P.M.

Signature of Parent/Guardian _____ Date _____

Form A-13

Notice of Rejection

(Note: If using this form as is, white out the form title at top before sending to child.)

Dear _____ ,

Thank you for applying to be a peer helper. I appreciate your interest in helping other students. Unfortunately, not all applicants could be selected because we had more applicants than spots for peer helpers this year. Please continue to help at our school in other areas.

Sincerely,

(Your Name Here)
Peer Helper Advisor

Form A-14

Teacher Request for Peer Helpers

To: Teachers, counselors, and administrators

From: (*Your Name Here*), Peer Helper Advisor

We are ready to begin our peer helping program for this year. The peer helpers will be trained to fulfill the following roles:

- **Peer Tutor:** Helps students who need academic assistance during the helper's lunch period.

- **Peer Mentor:** Role-models positive behavior and gives individual attention to primary-grade students. The older peer helper helps the younger helpee learn to make friends or learn to behave more appropriately on the playground. Mentoring takes place during the helpee's recess. It is important to realize that a peer helper will not be able to help a student whose behavior you yourself cannot control. Please don't refer such students to the program.

If you would like to have a peer helper work with one or more of your students, please fill in the request form below and return to me by (*Date Here*).

_____

Your Name _____

Grade _____ Room _____

Type of peer helper(s) requested (Circle one or both):   Peer Tutor   Peer Mentor

What in particular do you want the peer helper to work on? (This may change as the needs of your students change.)

Appendix B

Forms for
Training Peer Helpers

Checklist #1 for Initial Training Session

Pre-Training Preparation

Arrange these details well before the training session begins so that you can spend your training time focusing on the peer helpers.

☐ Request facilities. Arrange for bathroom, tables and chairs, and kitchen facilities if needed.

☐ Obtain adult supervisors and/or high school peer facilitators to help with group work.

☐ Order supplies.

☐ Meet with personnel ahead of time to give information about the training and to set expectations.

☐ Prearrange small groups of 5 to 7. Designate a high school peer facilitator or adult trainer to lead each group. I recommend that you do not allow your peer helpers to select their own groups. Mix 4th-, 5th-, and 6th-graders.

☐ Arrange for meals and snacks. Friday night is a potluck; make sure you have assigned peer helpers a dish to bring. Saturday you may arrange for pizza and punch if the PTA or student council sponsors the training. Have the students bring their own snacks.

☐ Make sure you have parent permission slips from all peer helpers.

 **Form B-2**

Checklist #2 for Initial Training Session

Training Personnel, Materials, and Meals/Snacks

Personnel
- ☐ 2 to 6 adult supervisors and/or high school facilitators
- ☐ 4th-, 5th, and 6th-grade peer helper trainees

Materials
For Each Participant

- ☐ pin-on nametag
- ☐ pocket folder with training packet handouts, including Forms B-6 through B-11 and three to four blank sheets of paper
- ☐ certificate of completion (Form B-12), to be given out at the end of the training

For Supply Table

- ☐ crayons (2 boxes per group)
- ☐ pencils (1 per participant)
- ☐ rulers/yardsticks (1-2 per group)
- ☐ scissors (2 per group)
- ☐ markers (2 boxes per group plus one for use in presentations)
- ☐ white construction paper (1 per participant)
- ☐ masking tape (1-2 rolls)
- ☐ white lined paper and envelope
- ☐ stapler and staples
- ☐ straight pins
- ☐ large white easel paper for facilitating discussion and for group posters
- ☐ tissues (1 box)
- ☐ colored dots
- ☐ camera/video recorder, film, and photographer (optional)

Room Preparation
In the middle of the room, arrange a circle of chairs. Around this circle, set up small group stations and label them red, yellow, blue, green, purple, (as many colors as you have groups).

Meals/Snacks
Friday

- ☐ Dinner (potluck or pizza)

Saturday

- ☐ Snack
- ☐ Lunch
- ☐ Afternoon snack

Tutoring and Mentoring

Agenda for Initial Training Session — Friday

Stick to the following schedule as much as possible. If you must eliminate an activity, make sure you don't eliminate ones essential for training goals. I recommend that you retain all of Friday's activities; if you must eliminate activities, choose from the Saturday agenda.

3:30 - 4:00 P.M.	**Room set-up; staff meeting**
4:00 - 5:15	**Ice-breaking activities; small group formation**

Signature Hunt

Purpose: To get to know each other

Materials: Copies of Signature Hunt Forms (Form B- 5)

Procedure: Give each student a Signature Hunt Form. Instruct them to go around the room, asking others to sign their names to one statement that is true for them. As signatures are exchanged, peer helpers begin to communicate with each other. Only one person may sign on each line. At the end of 15 minutes, students read their results. The winner has the most signatures. Only prize is a big hug.

Who Am I?

Purpose: To get to know each other

Procedure: Form a circle sitting on the floor. Circles should be limited to 15 to 20 people. One at a time, participants describe themselves using an adjective that begins with the letter of their first name. Then they say one thing they like to do with their friends. Example: "Nice Nancy, I love to dance." The second person repeats what the first person said and adds his or her own. Example: "Nice Nancy, I love to dance. Curious Calvin, I enjoy skating." Everyone has a turn. Allow 20 minutes for this activity.

Nametags

Nametags are important for training because they help everyone learn others' names. Peer helpers design their nametags during the Rules for Training discussion that follows. Make sure everyone wears one and that you collect them at the end of the day so they will be ready for the next morning.

Rules for Training

Lead a whole-group discussion about behavioral ground rules. You should write five to seven basic rules on newsprint and post on the wall. Include rules such as confidentiality, using good listening skills, not interrupting, etc. Make sure you spend adequate time on confidentiality, which is the first rule of peer helping.

Forming Small Groups

Announce who will be in each group. Let the leader call out the names. Each group is designated a certain color. These colors will be important for a later activity. Designate where each group is to meet.

5:15 - 6:00   **Dinner; sharing self**

Peer helpers break into triads for dinner. Instruct them to spend time with two others they do not know well. Information gathered during dinner will be used for after-dinner introductions. They are to find out something special that they would feel comfortable sharing with the whole group.

Dinner may be a potluck. If so, assign a course for each student, who should bring enough for six people. Let parents know as far ahead as possible.

6:00 - 6:15   **Introduction**

One triad at a time gets up and introduces other members of triad. They say something like, "This is my new friend John. The special thing I learned about him is _____." Applause is held until everyone is introduced.

6:15 - 6:45   **Small-Group Activity**

Me Shield

Purpose: Self-awareness

Materials: Me Shield activity sheet (Form B-6)

Procedure: Complete the information requested on the shields. Each group member shares what the shield represents for him or her.

6:45 - 7:00   **Whole-Group Discussion**

Ask participants what they think the purpose of peer helping is. Respond to their ideas as you write them on a chalkboard, flipchart or butcher block paper. Answer any questions that might come up. Generate your own official definition of what peer helping is.

7:00 - 7:15   **Small-Group Activity**

Let Go and Trust

Purpose: To build trust

Procedure: In small groups, students form a shoulder-to-shoulder circle. Only an inch or so should separate shoulders. One person at a time stands in the middle of the circle. Instruct those forming the circle that their job is to prevent the person in the middle from falling to the ground. They should be totally silent during this activity so that they can concentrate on their task. The person in the middle closes his or her eyes, folds arms across chest, and keeps feet together and stationary. Slowly, he or she leans back and trusts that the group will prevent a fall. As the person leans and is softly caught, he or she moves forward to the opposite side, where he or she is caught again. Each person gets a turn so they can experience what it's like to completely trust other people.

PEERS

7:15 - 7:45   **Activity**

Group Posters

Purpose: To build group spirit

Materials: white butcher paper, crayons, markers

Procedure: Students create a poster that symbolizes their small group. This can include items such as group name, group color, definition of peer helping, illustrations, motto, etc. Each small group stands in front of the whole group and explains their poster.

7:45 - 8:00   **Whole-Group Activity**

Self-assessment "I" Statements

Purpose: To clarify and reinforce training experience

Materials: None

Procedure: Ask peer helpers to share with the group what this part of the training has meant to them. Use the following as possible prompts:

- I learned that I...
- I learned that you...
- I want to...
- I need to learn to...
- I wonder...

8:00   **Dismissal**

Remind everyone to be punctual the next day. Collect nametags and packets. Remind them also not to share personal stories told by others, only the different activities they experienced. Introduce concept of confidentiality.

Agenda for Initial Training Session — Saturday

8:30 - 9:00 A.M. **Staff meeting; set-up for activities**

9:00 - 9:15 **Small Group Discussion**

Small groups discuss what was learned yesterday. Discuss the ideal atmosphere for learning. You might ask the following:

- What do you like teachers to do?
- What don't you like teachers to do?
- How do you feel about praise, positive feedback, non-verbals?

Generate a model for good teaching they can use for peer helping.

9:15 - 9:45 **Whole-Group Activity**

We're Sticking Together

Purpose: To learn about non-verbal communication (body language) and to increase empathy for outsiders

Materials: 4 to 5 colors of dot decals

Procedure: Randomly stick one colored dot on each child's forehead. Do not allow the child to see what color it is. Each person must find his or her color group without any verbalization. Only body language such as eye contact, pointing, nodding or other head movement may be used. One person has a dot that doesn't match anybody else's. After color groups have found each other, discuss what it feels like to be left out.

9:45 - 10:30 **Whole-Group Activity**

"I Am Lovable and Capable" (IALAC)

Purpose: To examine the relationship between self-concept and the way one communicates; and to help students become more aware of the impact of their words and actions on others.

Materials: paper, pencils

Procedure:

1. Take a sheet of paper and write the letters I-A-L-A-C on it in bold print. Hold this to your chest so that the students can see it. Tell them the following:

"Everyone carries an invisible IALAC sign around with them at all times and wherever they go. IALAC stands for 'I Am Lovable and Capable.' This is our *self-concept*, or, how we feel about ourselves. How good we feel about ourselves is often affected by how others interact with us. If someone is nasty to us, teases us, puts us down, rejects us, hits us, etc., then a piece of our IALAC sign is destroyed."

Tutoring and Mentoring

Illustrate this by tearing a corner piece off the sign. Then continue:

"I am going to tell you a story to illustrate how this happens in everyday life."

2. Proceed to tell the students about a boy or girl who is about the same age they are. Pick a name no one in the class has. Try to be dramatic as you tell the story. Below is an outline of the story. You will have to fill in, using your imagination. Have the high school leaders or adult leaders act out the story in skit form. As you describe each event that negatively affects the student's IALAC sign, tear another piece off the sign until at the end you are left with almost nothing.

"Michael is still lying in bed three minutes after his alarm goes off. All of a sudden his mother calls to him, 'Michael, you lazy-head, get your body out of bed and get down here before I send your father up there.' (*Rip!*) Michael gets out of bed and goes to get dressed but can't find a clean pair of socks. His mother tells him he'll have to wear yesterday's pair. (*Rip!*) He goes to brush his teeth and his older sister, who has already locked herself in the bathroom, tells him to drop dead. (*Rip!*) He goes to breakfast and finds soggy cereal waiting for him. (*Rip!*) He goes to school, he forgets his lunch, and his mother calls to him, 'Michael, you have forgotten your lunch. You'd forget your head if it weren't attached!' (*Rip!*) As he gets to the corner, he sees the school bus pull away and so he has to walk to school. (*Rip!*) He's late and has to get a pass from the principal, who gives him a lecture. (*Rip!*) When he gets to class, his teacher calls on him with a question Michael can't answer. (*Rip!*)

3. Continue the story through the school day with appropriate examples. Some possibilities are:

- Making a mistake in reading so that all the kids laugh

- Being picked last to play basketball during gym

- Dropping his tray in the lunchroom and everyone applauding

- Being referred to as "Hey you" in class

4. Turn the story around at this point, replacing the pieces of the IALAC sign as Michael begins to receive positive communications and kind words from those he encountered throughout his day.

"Just as Michael is ready to leave school for the day, something different happens. Before he walks out of class, his teacher apologizes for putting him on the spot. In the hallway he passes the principal, who comments that she's heard Michael has done a terrific job on his science project."

Continue putting the sign back together as you tell the story, until it is completely restored. Use more positive experiences such as:

- Getting invited to an after-school activity by the kids who laughed at him earlier.

- Being greeted at the front door by his sister, who gives him a friendly smile and hug.

• Receiving praise from his mother, who tells him how proud she is to be his mom.

5. After the skit, have a short whole-group discussion about the effects of negative communications, even if such types of comments are meant "in fun."

6. Give each peer helper a large piece of white construction paper, pencil, crayons, and markers. Invite them to design their own IALAC sign, which will be theirs to keep. Below the letters I-A-L-A-C, they should write out the words "I Am Loving and Capable."

10:30 - 10:45	**Break**
10:45 - 11:00	**Small-Group Activity**

Who Am I?

Using the same groups that played this game on Friday night, repeat the game to see if the group can remember the adjectives and special thing the participants like to do.

11:00 - 11:30   Whole-Group Discussion: How to Tutor/How to Mentor

Refer the students to the How to Tutor/How to Mentor handout (Form B-7). Lead discussion based on this information.

11:30 - 12:15 P.M.   Lunch with Two New People

Tell the students that the PTA has sponsored a pizza and drink lunch for your program. Instruct them to eat with two people whom they have not yet gotten to know.

12:15 - 12:30   Small-Group Activity

Let Go and Trust

Play this game again to see if the trust level has increased.

12:30 - 1:00   Small-Group Activity

Remember the Time

Purpose: To increase sensitivity to others' needs

Materials: piece of paper folded into four squares and pencil/pen

Procedure: Instruct small groups to recall four special times in their past based on the questions below. Ask them to draw a picture or write sentences about those times in each of the four squares in their paper. Allow 2-3 minutes for each memory.

• Remember the time you felt very loved. Who made you feel that way? What did he or she do that made you feel loved?

• Remember the time you were successful at something. What was it?

• Remember the time you were very giving. What did you do?

Tutoring and Mentoring

> - Remember the time you received something from someone. How did that feel?

After everyone is finished, each person shares their responses with other group members.

1:00 - 1:30　　**Whole-Group Discussion: Do's and Don'ts of Peer Helping.**

Refer the students to their training packet handout (Form B-8). Discuss any points that need explanation.

1:30 - 2:00　　**Skits**

Each small group puts together a skit that shows what has happened in the training. The skit will be presented to parents at 4:45. The skits should not be longer than five minutes.

2:00 - 2:15　　**Break**

2:15 - 2:30　　**Whole-Group Activity**

I Am Special

Purpose: To help helpers focus on the purpose of training

Procedure: Participants form a large circle, holding hands. One by one, each says his or her name and shares with the whole group one thing that is special about him or her. Then go around the group a second time, having each person share one thing they learned in training that will help them grow.

2:30 - 2:45　　**Whole-Group Discussion**

The purpose of this discussion will be to focus on social skills and how to be a positive role-model. Ask small groups to generate a list of appropriate social skills that grade-school children should develop. Then generate a list of inappropriate social behaviors. Have them think about ways to move their helpees toward more appropriate behaviors. Group leaders give feedback.

2:45 - 3:15　　**Whole-Group Activity**

Letter to Self

Purpose: To focus on goals

Materials: paper and pencil

Procedure: Instruct helpers to go off by themselves to write a letter in which they describe their goals for this year. These goals should include personal goals, school goals, and peer helper program goals. After finishing, they should fold the paper, put their name on the outside, and staple it. When you have received all the letters, keep them and return them to the students at the end of the year for their review.

3:15 - 3:45　　**Procedures for Peer Helpers**

Return to the large group. Explain scheduling procedures, referral procedures, and helper/helpee match-up procedures. Go over the Code of Ethics and their Log Sheets (Forms B-9 and B-10). Explain their relationships to helpees, teachers and parents.

PEERS **3:45-4:00**   **Small-Group Activity**

Numbers in Order

Purpose: To develop trust in each other and learn cooperation

Procedure: Form circles of 10-12 participants holding hands. The group must count from one to ten (if 12 in group, count to 12). Participants, in no pre-determined order, say one number at a time, starting at 1 and building toward the target number. The catch is that no one knows who will say the next number. If two or more people say the same number simultaneously, the game is over and you start again. No communication, verbal or non-verbal, is allowed. The object is to reach the target number without two or more people saying the same number.

4:00 - 4:20   **Skit Practice**

4:20 - 4:45   **Awarding of Certificates; Question & Answers; Cleanup**

Hand out certificates (Form B-12) and answer any remaining questions they may have. Have the students start helping you clean up before their parents arrive.

4:45 - 5:00   **Parents Arrive**

Students fill out their evaluation forms (Form B-11). They present their skits for parents. Session is dismissed.

5:00 - 5:30   **Cleanup**

Form B-5

Signature Hunt Form

Find people who fit the descriptions below and have them sign their names on the appropriate line.

I was born in another state. _____

I am wearing contact lenses. _____

I have traveled outside the United States. _____

I was born the same month as you. _____

I have never had a cavity. _____

I am wearing white socks. _____

I have played a violin. _____

I play tennis. _____

I am wearing shoes that tie. _____

I watch TV less than six hours per week. _____

I thinks sports are a waste of time. _____

I have had surgery. _____

My parents own a red car. _____

I have a pet bird. _____

I know how to play chess. _____

I just started our school this year. _____

PEERS

Me Shield

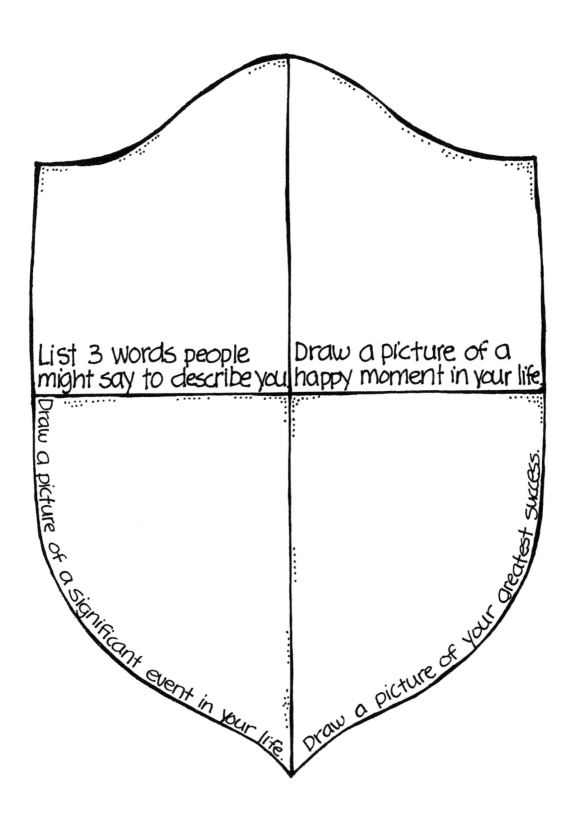

List 3 words people might say to describe you.

Draw a picture of a happy moment in your life.

Draw a picture of a significant event in your life.

Draw a picture of your greatest success.

How to Tutor/How to Mentor

How to Tutor

- Young children like structure. Try to follow the same routine every session until the helpee feels comfortable.

- Make sure you use your helpee's name when you are with him or her.

- Give positive feedback as much as possible. It's very important for young children to feel special.

- Give clear directions.

- Make sure you understand what you're supposed to be doing with the helpee.

- If the helpee isn't cooperating, talk to the receiving teacher or to the advisor about finding ways to solve the problem.

- Start a session off with easy questions and work up to harder ones.

- Never resort to putdowns or threats. Remember how important you are to the helpee.

- Be enthusiastic.

How to Mentor

- Interact with your buddy on the playground by involving him or her in fun games and activities.

- Try to get your helpee involved with other kids his or her age.

- Have conversations in which you and your helpee discuss how to get along with others. Conversation is as important as your play interaction.

- Sometimes your helpee may not feel like playing with you. Respect his or her right to choose. Try to think of ways to establish the relationship so that the helpee isn't withdrawn from you.

- Don't develop a relationship in which you and your helpee play exclusively with each other.

- Don't discipline the helpee. If he or she misbehaves, refer the matter to a responsible adult.

Your First Meeting with Your Helpee

- Introduce yourself. As the first meeting may be awkward, talk about yourself to reduce the tension. This situation will improve with time.

- Ask why the student thinks he or she needs a peer helper.

- Define your role with the helpee: the schedule, what you'll be doing, etc.

- State your desire to help and be available for the person.

Do's and Don'ts for Peer Helpers

- Do interact with younger students by engaging them in games and fun activities.
- Do follow through on your commitments to the person who needs your help.
- Do maintain your own good grades and good relationships.
- Do reach out and help others become successful.
- Do accept people as they are.
- Do listen and pay attention.
- Do give support and encouragement.
- Do realize that not all problems can be solved and not all people want to be helped.
- Do refer serious problems to a professional at school.
- Do be available.
- Do listen between the lines.
- Do be genuine and sincere.
- Do respect other people's need for privacy.

- Don't judge people.
- Don't put people down.
- Don't gossip about what is said during peer helping sessions.
- Don't expect all problems to be solved quickly and easily.
- Don't argue.

Peer Helper's Code of Ethics

- I will have respect for the people I help.

- I will keep confidentiality at all times except in situations where there is a threat to the safety of others.

- I will not give advice but will only offer possible solutions.

- I will refer a helpee to a responsible adult if there is a problem.

Log Sheet/Record of Activities

Peer Helper _____

Keep this log sheet in your peer helping folder. It will collected and reviewed periodically.

Date	Time	Activity	Helpee(s) Name(s)

Peer Helper Training Evaluation

What I liked best about the training was

What I liked least about the training was

Participant's Certificate

(Note: Photocopy the certificate on the reverse on parchment or similar paper, using your own peer helping logo if you wish.)

PEERS

I CAN MAKE A DIFFERENCE

PEERS

This certifies that

_____

has successfully completed the

Peer Helper Training at

_____ **School.**

Given this day, _____.

_____
Peer Helper Trainer

_____
Peer Helper Advisor

Appendix C

Forms for Evaluating Your Program

Teacher Evaluation Form

To: Teachers

From: (*Your Name Here*), Peer Helper Advisor

Re: Peer Helping Program Feedback

This is the first year that the peer helper program has been used in our school. Therefore, your honest evaluation will provide valuable insight to both our school and other schools in the district. Your responses will be used to improve the effectiveness of this program next year.

Please take a few minutes to respond to the questions and return the form to me by (*Date Here*).

Thank you for a successful year! Your support and encouragement have helped this program to be a success.

This evaluation is divided into four sections: Peer Helper Improvement, Helpee Improvement, Student Attitudes, and Your Attitudes. Please skip any section that does not apply to you. Feel free to write out any additional comments, praises, and/or suggestions for improvement and attach them to this form.

For all sections, please circle the number that best represents your response to each statement. Explain your response or give an example in the extra space in the right margin. Use the following chart in rating each statement:

0 = Does not apply
1 = No change
2 = Very little change
3 = Some change
4 = Large change
5 = Very large change

Section 1: Peer Helper Improvement

Have the peer helpers benefited from the program?

As a result of participating in the peer helping program, my students have shown improvement in their:

1. Enthusiasm for attending school.   5 4 3 2 1 0

2. Positive attitude about themselves.   5 4 3 2 1 0

3. Ability to get along with other children.   5 4 3 2 1 0

4. Academic skills
   (i.e., reading, spelling math, etc.)   5 4 3 2 1 0

5. Social skills (i.e., making friends,
   displaying acceptable playground
   and classroom behavior, etc.)   5 4 3 2 1 0

6. Ability to make responsible decisions.   5 4 3 2 1 0

Section 2: Helpee Improvement

Have the students who were helped benefited from the program?

As a result of participating in the peer helper program,
my students have shown improvement in their:

1. Enthusiasm for attending school.   5 4 3 2 1 0

2. Positive attitude about themselves.   5 4 3 2 1 0

3. Ability to get along with other children.   5 4 3 2 1 0

4. Academic skills (i.e., reading, math, etc.)   5 4 3 2 1 0

5. Social skills (i.e., making friends,
   displaying acceptable playground
   and classroom behavior, etc.)   5 4 3 2 1 0

6. Ability to make responsible decisions.   5 4 3 2 1 0

Section 3: Student Attitudes

What do the students think of the program?

The **peer helpers** reported that they enjoyed...

...the helpees they were paired with.   5 4 3 2 1 0

...helping students with academic skills
    (math, reading, spelling, etc.)   5 4 3 2 1 0

...helping students with social skills
    (making friends, playing well, etc.)   5 4 3 2 1 0

The **helpees** reported that they enjoyed...

...the helper they were paired with.   5 4 3 2 1 0

...being helped with academic skills
    (math, reading, spelling, etc.)   5 4 3 2 1 0

...being helped with social skills
    (making friends, playing well, etc.)   5 4 3 2 1 0

Section 4: Your Attitudes

What do I think of the peer helper program?

1. The peer helper application and
   selection process was reasonable.   5 4 3 2 1 0

2. The initial training session and the
   biweekly training meetings were
   successful at providing the skills
   to be an effective peer helper.   5 4 3 2 1 0

3. The preparation of materials for the
   peer helper initial training session
   was easy for me to complete.   5 4 3 2 1 0

4. The peer helper program should be
   continued next year at our school.   5 4 3 2 1 0

Tutoring and Mentoring

Parent/Guardian Evaluation Form

(For parent/guardian of child who received help from peer helpers.)

Dear Parent/Guardian,

This is the first year that the peer helper program has been used in our school. Therefore, your honest evaluation will provide valuable insight to both our school and other schools in the district. Your responses will be used to improve the effectiveness of this program next year.

Please take a few minutes to respond to the questions and return this form to me in Room (*Number Here*) on (*Date Here*). Or return it to your child's teacher by (*Date Here*).

Thank you for a successful year! Your support and encouragement have helped this program to be a success.

Sincerely,

(*Your Name Here*)
Peer Helper Advisor

Please circle the number that best represents your response to each statement. Use the chart below in rating each statement. Explain your response or give an example in the extra space in the right margin.

0 = Does not apply
1 = No opinion
2 = Strongly disagree
3 = Disagree
4 = Agree
5 = Strongly agree

As a result of participating in the peer helping program my child has shown improvement in his/her:

1. Enthusiasm for attending school. 5 4 3 2 1 0

2. Positive attitude about him/herself. 5 4 3 2 1 0

3. Ability to get along with other children. 5 4 3 2 1 0

4. Academic skills (i.e., reading, math, etc.) 5 4 3 2 1 0

5. Social skills (i.e., making friends,
   displaying acceptable playground
   and classroom behavior, etc.) 5 4 3 2 1 0

6. Ability to make responsible decisions. 5 4 3 2 1 0

---

7. My child reported that he/she liked the peer helper he/she was paired with.   5 4 3 2 1 0

8. My child reported that he/she liked attending the after-school tutoring sessions.   5 4 3 2 1 0

9. My child reported that he/she liked working with a peer helper on social skills.   5 4 3 2 1 0

10. The time commitment was reasonable.   5 4 3 2 1 0

11. The peer helper program should be continued next year at our school.   5 4 3 2 1 0

12. Next year, if my child shows a need for improvement in social skills, I will recommend that he/she participate in the peer helper program again.   5 4 3 2 1 0

13. Next year, if my child shows a need for improvement in academic skills, I will recommend that he/she participate in the peer helper program again.   5 4 3 2 1 0

Please add any additional comments, praises, and/or suggestions for improvement:

Peer Helper Evaluation Form

Please fill out the following survey.

Did you like being a peer helper? (Circle one.) Yes   No

Would you recommend the peer helping program to your friends? Yes   No

What did you like most about the program?

What didn't you like about the program?

If you could change one thing about the peer helping program, what would it be?

Write down any other comments here:

Resources

Books and Journal Articles

Cihak, Mary K., and Barbara Heron. *Games Children Should Play.* Glenview, Illinois: Scott, Foresman and Co., Glenview, 1980.

Foster, E. S. *Tutoring: Learning by Helping.* Minneapolis: Educational Media Corporation, 1983.

Gray, H. D., and J. Tindall. *Peer Counseling: An In-depth Look at Training Peer Helpers.* Muncie, Indiana: Accelerated Development, Inc., 1985.

Kriedler, William. *Creative Conflict Resolution.* Glenview, Ilinois: Scott, Foresman and Co., 1984.

Maslow, A. H. *Toward A Psychology of Being.* 2nd ed. New York: Van Nostrand Reinhold, 1968.

Myrick, R. D. "Peer Helpers: The Helping Hands of School Counselors." *The Peer Facilitator Quarterly* (September 1992): 8.

Myrick, R. D., and R. P. Bowman. *Becoming a Friendly Helper: A Handbook for Student Facilitators.* Minneapolis: Educational Media Corporation, 1981.

Myrick, R. D., and T. Erney. *Youth Helping Youth: A Handbook for Training Peer Facilitators.* Minneapolis: Educational Media Corp, 1979.

Rogers, C. H. *A Way of Being.* Boston: Houghton Mifflin, 1980.

Samuels, D., and M. Samuels. *The Complete Handbook of Peer Counseling.* Miami: Fiesta Publishing, 1975.

Sturkie, Joan, and Marsh Cassady. *Acting It Out Junior: Discussion Starters for 10-13 Year Olds.* San Jose, California: Resource Publications, Inc., 1992.

Sturkie, Joan, and Valerie Gibson. *The Peer Helper's Pocketbook*. San Jose, California: Resource Publications, Inc., 1992.

Varenhorst, B. B. *Curriculum Guide for Student Peer Counseling*. Palo Alto, California: Barbara Varenhorst Peer Counseling Program (25 Churchill Avenue, Palo Alto, CA 94306), 1980.

Tutoring Materials

Workbooks

Hall, Nancy, and R. Price. *Explode the Code: A Phonetically-Based Reading System*. Cambridge, Massachussetts: Educators Publishing Service, Inc.

Villalpando, Eleanor. *English Workbook*. Scottsdale, Arizona: Remedia Publications.

Software

Math Invaders: Computer Game for the Memorization of Math Facts. Rochester, New York: Winners Circle Education Company.

Math Word Problems: Weekly Reader Software. Norfolk, Connecticut: Optimum Resource, Inc.

Resources for Drama & Storytelling

STORYTELLING STEP-BY-STEP

Marsh Cassady

Paper, $9.95
168 pages, 5½" x 8½"
ISBN 0-89390-183-0

In this basic handbook, Marsh Cassady breaks down the elements needed for successful storytelling. Learn how to adapt a story for a particular audience and how to hold that audience's attention; how to choose a story that matches the occasion; and how to use voice, gesture and props.

CREATING STORIES FOR STORYTELLING

Marsh Cassady

Paper, $9.95
168 pages, 5½" x 8½"
ISBN 0-89390-205-5

Whether you're a storyteller or a storywriter, this book will show you how to create better stories. The key, says the author, is analysis. Each chapter will help you discover your own style of telling or writing; excerpts from over twenty stories will give you ideas for creating the right story for your audience.

ACTING STEP-BY-STEP

Marsh Cassady

Paper, $9.95
192 pages, 5½" x 8½"
ISBN 0-89390-120-2

Acting Step-by-Step teaches you how to apply your creativity to situations where knowledge of acting is essential. For every field of work—from politics to policy, from management to ministry, and, of course, for acting—this book will give you new insights on improving your presentation/performance.

PLAYWRITING STEP-BY-STEP

Marsh Cassady

Paper, $11.95
120 pages, 5½" x 8½"
ISBN 0-89390-056-7

With chapters devoted to plot, character, dialog, genre, writing, and marketing your play, this book is a comprehensive guide for the writer who is bursting with ideas but needs to learn how to develop them.

Order from your bookseller, or use the form on the next page.

Discussion Starters for Students!

ACTING IT OUT
74 Short Plays for Starting Discussions with Teenagers

Joan Sturkie &
Marsh Cassady, PhD

Paper, $21.95
368 pages, 6" x 9"
ISBN 0-89390-178-4

Getting teenagers to talk about how they're feeling can be frustrating. *Acting It Out* offers a role-playing approach: Teens read or act out a short play, then discuss how the characters deal with the particular issue. The provided questions help teens address their own issues and feelings. These dramas address challenging subjects: AIDS, abortion, suicide, child abuse, gangs, and more. Ideal for peer counseling groups or for any class or situation in which values discussions are appropriate.

ACTING IT OUT JUNIOR
Discussion Starters for 10-13 Year Olds

Joan Sturkie &
Marsh Cassady, PhD

Paper, $15.95
264 pages, 6" x 9"
ISBN 0-89390-240-3

The short dramas in this book are designed to open up avenues for self-discovery and to prepare young people to make decisions about their lives. After role-playing a drama, use the discussion questions to help your students explore their reactions and feelings about the topic addressed.

- -

Order Form

Order these resources from your local bookstore, or mail this form to:

QTY	TITLE	PRICE	TOTAL

Subtotal: _____

CA residents add 7¼% sales tax
(Santa Clara Co. residents, 8¼%): _____

Postage and handling
($2 for orders up to $20; 10% of orders over $20 but
less than $150; $15 for orders of $150 or more): _____

Total: _____

Resource Publications, Inc.
160 E. Virginia Street #290
San Jose, CA 95112-5876
(408) 286-8505
(408) 287-8748 FAX

☐ My check or money order is enclosed.
☐ Charge my ☐ VISA ☐ MC.

Expiration Date_____

Card # _____-_____-_____-_____

Signature _____

Name (print) _____

Institution _____

Street _____

City/State/ZIP _____

TM